# THIS BOOK

## SCOTT PHILLIP WEBER PA
### Franchise Legal Solutions℠

*"At Franchise Legal Solutions, we are committed to helping entrepreneurs expand their businesses. We focus on helping them grow through franchising, licensing, and multi-unit development. If you think your company has the potential to go regional, national, or global, we would be honored to meet with you."*

*- Scott Phillip Weber, P.A.*

*(813) 337-6650*

*www.FranchiseLegalSolutions.com*
*3709 W. McKay Avenue Tampa, FL 33609*

KEVIN HARRINGTON AND DANIEL PRIESTLEY

# KEY PERSON
## *of* INFLUENCE

FOREWORD BY TOPHER MORRISON

**The Five-Step Method** *to become one of the most highly valued and highly paid people in your industry*

# RETHINK PRESS

First published in Great Britain 2015

by Rethink Press (www.rethinkpress.com)

© Copyright Kevin Harrington and Daniel Priestley

Cover image © Entrevo Pte Ltd

Illustrations: Andrew Priestley

# WHAT OTHERS ARE SAYING

'This book has very powerful ideas that will have you achieving much more in far less time. Hard work is not enough; if you want to make it big, you must strive to become a Key Person of Influence. This book shows you exactly how to do that faster.'

Mike Harris
Creator of three multi-billion pound businesses and Author of *Find Your Lightbulb*.

'Why be a "worker bee" when you could instead be a "Key Person of Influence"? Daniel's book explains exactly how to get into the inner circle of any industry, fast. Read this book!'

Mike Southon
*Financial Times* Columnist and best-selling Business Author.

I dedicate this book to my late father, my first and best mentor.

**Kevin Harrington**

I dedicate this book to the people who have used their power of influence to improve the world. To those of you who think about the future and act now, I hope that the ideas in this book assist you in creating a world that works for everyone.

**Daniel Priestley**

# CONTENTS

# FOREWORD

Since the launch of the Key Person of Influence first edition in the UK, almost five years ago, over 20,000 entrepreneurs around the world have read this book, implemented the strategies, and increased their status as a person of influence in their community and their market.

The notion of being a key person of influence is appealing to the majority of business owners – the savvy ones, anyway. But I don't want you to read this book as a "how to become" a key person of influence. I want you to read it from the notion of "how to become more of" a key person of influence. No matter how influential you are, there is always a greater sphere of influence for you to impact.

If you are already a key person of influence in your market, how can you expand your market reach?

If you are already a key person of influence in your community, how can you expand that influence to your city, or state, or region?

If you are reading this book, I can safely predict that you realize you can either expand your market further, shorten your sales cycle, or increase your rates. Hopefully, you are the kind of entrepreneur who wants all three.

The information in this book isn't hyperbole, or anecdotal. It's tried and tested. And, even more, it's not magical or secret. The principles in this book are grounded in traditional business practices that have been around for many years. Where this book will give you the greatest increase in entrepreneurial horsepower will be if you implement the steps in the order Daniel and Kevin lay out. If I say "Bob owns the business" – that has a very specific meaning. And that's much different than saying, "the business owns Bob". Same words, used in a different order, create a remarkably different result. And therein lies the key to getting the most from this book – implementing the steps in the correct order.

When I speak about the principles of becoming a key person of influence, I hear people all the time say things like, "I already do that, I have an e-book" or "I already know this stuff, I have lots of videos online." These people just don't get it. They are usually the kind of entrepreneur who says everything is going great in their business and they put on an amazing front, but have no real sales to back up their boastfulness. Writing a book won't make you a key person of influence. Neither will videos on YouTube or getting on TV or even teaming up with people more successful than you. Here's a perfect example:

Writing a book that everyone would benefit from clearly indicates that you haven't yet established a powerful pitch that speaks to a specific target audience. And until you take that first step – clearly articulating your target market – how can you write an effective book?

So take heed. If you find yourself saying, "Oh, I already do that" while reading this book, ask yourself if you have done the other steps previously described? Because, if not, you haven't fully taken advantage of the great things you are already doing inside your business.

This book isn't just about giving you a roadmap to more efficient and profitable sales; it's also a clear-cut roadmap to how you can do business with us in the future, as well. Key Person of Influence, whether it's in the U.K., Australia, Singapore, or the U.S., is known for establishing powerful partnerships with influential business leaders. When we look for partners, we look for how they measure up in the five key indicators that you are going to read about in this book. One way to measure the effectiveness of this book, and provide additional insights as to what parts you need to focus on the most, would be to take our free, 4-minute influence scorecard. This evaluation will have you answer 40 yes/no questions and then give you a quantifiable measurement on how you stack up with you level of influence in your market. You can take the scorecard here:

http://www.keypersonofinfluence.com/scorecard

I want you to think of the word "influence." What does this mean to you? For most, they see this word as a verb. It's something you do to someone. Make no mistake – at Key Person of Influence we don't see this word as a verb. It's a noun. It's your entrepreneurial mojo – an essence about you that, when you have influence, people are attracted to you. Have you ever wondered why, for some entrepreneurs, business comes easy, and others seem to struggle? It's the influence they possess. When you have it, you become irresistible. Objections become questions to move forward, and to the uneducated, they just think you are lucky. It's not luck, it's influence. And the authors of this book have it in spades.

Daniel Priestley is the quintessential entrepreneur. Totally unemployable and a natural problem solver. He is the genius behind the 5-step process to becoming a highly-valued, and highly-paid key person of influence in your market. There has never been a lunch or dinner, or a time when we are rock-climbing in London at The Castle, where I'm not blown away by something Daniel says. What seems mysterious to me is just common sense to him. The next best thing to listening to Daniel over dinner is reading his words in this book. By the end, you will feel like you know him, that you connect with him, and you will want to meet him. That's influence.

Kevin Harrington is a living legend. A man who practically invented an industry called infomercial, and, without ever knowing Daniel, had all five steps in place in his businesses. The result? He's sold over $5 billion dollars' worth of products and that number is still rising. Harvard and MIT have dedicated entire courses to learning how to run a business "The Kevin Harrington Way". As one of the original sharks on the US television show *Shark Tank*, his public persona exploded. But what many people don't realize is how he was already an industry titan in his market long before *Shark Tank*. As you read through his personal stories in this book, you will soon realize that *Shark Tank* wasn't nearly as impressive as his previous accomplishments.

One last thought before you begin reading. If you don't have a pen within reach, go get one. Because this won't be a book you read through once and put on a shelf. This book, if you really get the ideas presented, will inspire you to write notes on the side, dog ear the key pages, and circle the topics for quick reference over and over. Enjoy your path to becoming an even greater key person of influence.

**Topher Morrison**
**Managing Director, KPI USA**

# INTRODUCTION

## Highly valued, highly paid and having fun

At the center of every industry, you will find an inner circle of people who are the most well-known and highly valued people. They are the Key People of Influence. You probably already know of these people in your industry:

*Their names come up in conversation... for all the right reasons.*

*They attract a lot of opportunities... the right sort.*

*They earn a more money than most... and it isn't a struggle.*

*They can make a project successful if they are involved... and people know it.*

Key People of Influence enjoy a special status in their chosen field because they are well connected, well known, well regarded and highly valued. They get invited to be a part of the best teams and projects, and they can often write their own terms. Key People of Influence also have more fun. They get invited on trips. People buy them dinner and drinks. They are treated with respect and others listen when they speak. These people are in demand; they don't chase opportunities, they create them.

People think that it must take years or decades to become a Key Person of Influence (KPI). They think that KPIs need degrees or doctorates. They think KPIs must be gifted or from wealthy families. But they are wrong. While time invested, qualifications, talents and a wealthy family are helpful, they are not a reliable way to make yourself a Key Person of Influence. There are plenty of people who have been in an industry for years who are *not* a Key

Person of Influence. There are plenty of MBAs and PhDs who are not yet KPIs. There are people with talent and people born into privileged families who aren't KPIs either. And then there are unusual stories like Kevin Harrington.

Kevin was born to a normal family, had a normal education and grew up with the usual challenges most of us have experienced. Nothing about his past would lead you to expect he would go on to build a business with multi-billion dollar revenues, create the world's leading entrepreneur network (EO), become a best-selling author, a celebrity, a highly-paid speaker and an award-winning businessman. But he did. And along the way, he created dozens of millionaires, made several people into household names and helped to raise money for important charities. In the high-intensity world of direct sales and television shopping, he built a thirty-year reputation as one of the most fair and professional people in his industry.

How did he become so wealthy, successful and influential? He did the five things you'll see explained in this book.

Kevin met me and read my Key Person of Influence method and instantly said, "That's how I did it!" And what's more, he said, "That's the formula for how almost everyone does it!" It's certainly how I built my success.

I started with very little and built a global business turning over millions, all before the age of thirty. I've made deals in Australia, USA, Asia and Europe, and discovered that the method in this book is powerful wherever you go.

People all over the world respond to the KPI Method that you'll learn in coming chapters. It's a method based on clearly communicating your value and packaging it up in a way the market finds desirable. The principles in this book have been tested across fifty different industries, in over a dozen countries, by over 1000 entrepreneurs and leaders, and they have proven to be universal.

> *It's not difficult to become a Key Person of Influence within your industry in the next twelve months if you take the steps set out in this book in the order they are prescribed and implement them at a high standard.*

If you do, you won't need to go back to school or spend decades climbing corporate ladders. You will quickly become a Key Person of Influence in your field.

You will never fear not having money or influence again.

You will already have everything you will ever need.

# ①

# THE WORLD HAS CHANGED AND SO MUST YOU

*We are living in a very different world today than we were just a decade ago. We're at the beginning of a whole new era. We are no longer in the Industrial Age; we are in a new economy that's digital, global, intangible, more meaningful and very entrepreneurial. Everything has changed and so must you.*

## Looking good, going nowhere

There's an accountant I know who's feeling frustrated. He is a great accountant, yet he's not happy; and I know why. When he was eighteen years old, fresh out of high school, he thought the smartest thing to do would be to train to be an accountant. He was good at math and economics and it made sense at the time to study and get into accounting.

Today he's frustrated. He's brilliant at what he does, but he still has to compete on price. Like most of the people in his industry, he thinks that the key to making more money is continuing to learn more about the technical aspects of his job. Unfortunately for him, everyone in his business is focused on getting more qualifications, and he finds himself constantly playing catch-up. Regardless of how much he earns, he still feels that he is only slightly ahead of the game.

Lately, he's been questioning everything; he feels that his life today is based upon the best thinking of an eighteen-year-old. He has lived out seventeen years of this teenager's decision. Now he's in his late-thirties, his values have shifted and so has the world. He now competes with software, accountants in India and his own mindset, about how his industry "should be."

His story isn't unique; I hear it all the time. Many people are great at what they do, but don't feel fulfilled. They begin to feel that life is passing by year-by-year and their goals haven't been realized. Maybe this has happened to you. You might have even started questioning whether you made the right career choices or even life choices.

By the end of this book, you are going to see that you don't need to turn your life upside down. You don't need to go back to school. You can forget the MBA and the PhD if you want. You can forget the get-rich-quick schemes that take you off track. If you follow what I am about to tell you in this book, you will become a Key Person of Influence in your industry within the next six to twelve months. You'll enjoy yourself more, you'll make more money and it won't take you more time. You will even feel more sure of yourself.

However, before I begin to share with you some of the actions that need to be taken, we must first face up to some facts. We are living in a different world. It's not the same as it used to be. There are some new concepts you need to embrace and some old ideas you need to let go of quickly.

If you are willing to do that, then let's begin the journey.

## Your best thinking five years ago is your baggage today

In the last few years we have seen the explosive growth of social media, online shopping, massive breakthroughs in technology, a global recession, globalization and a massive shift towards entrepreneurship over employment. In the last few years, we have seen the economy change, the environment change, developing nations stride forward and the collective mindset of the world radically shift. All in just a few short years.

Given these changes, your best thinking from five years ago is your baggage today. Any decisions you made back then about your career, the location you lived, the technology you used, the people you associated with, and the thought leaders you followed were all based upon a world that no longer exists. Software we purchased five years ago for ten thousand dollars or more has been superseded by free, cloud-based software today, and what we dreamed of doing five years ago costs fifty dollars a month on subscription!

Entrepreneurs who were admired five years ago but didn't shift their business model have lost their fortunes. Many experts of five years ago are now scratching their heads. Great leaders from five years ago have teams who aren't performing. Customers now expect to get for free the things they would have paid for five years ago. Products that used to be available only through retail are now freely available online. Countries that offered the best opportunities for wealth creation five years ago are struggling with debt. The poor countries of the previous decade are powerhouses of enterprise.

Unless we can let go of everything we currently think and do, we will fail to see the opportunities of tomorrow. The temptation is to throw everything away. However at the core of who you are and what you do is a raw essence that has always powered you. You need to strip back to that core and create new ways to express yourself.

When Steve Jobs took over Apple in 1997, one of his first decisions was to get rid of the Apple Museum that occupied the foyer when people walked through the front door. He said that he refused to be in a company that was living in its past. He believed at the core of Apple was vision, boldness and innovation. He knew the essence

of Apple was thinking differently and combining art with technology. If he couldn't strip away everything but that, the future was going to be dire. He didn't want the future of the company to be affected by the best thinking of its history. He wanted it to be living up to the best thinking of the future.

It's time to draw a line in the sand; to take some time out and ask yourself what is at your core. Ask yourself this question:

> *"If I was starting completely fresh, in a world where anything is possible, what would I love to be doing?"*

We haven't asked you what you should be doing. We've asked you what you would *love* to be doing. If you are like most people, your passionate purpose is a lot closer than you think.

There are parts of your business that you love, parts that drain your energy and maybe even parts you hate. Maybe you have a hobby you love, but the job you hate keeps you from it; look for the clues that are hidden in that hobby.

This book will reveal to you exactly how you can position yourself as a Key Person of Influence (KPI) in your field within the next twelve months. As a result, you will attract opportunities, connections, ideas and resources that mean you will be able to do what you love and get paid what you are worth.

In this new, exciting, changing world, you will discover that it's people and teams who love what they do that are thriving. If it feels like hard work, you will always get trumped by the people who have a passion for it.

Your passion and vitality are an asset in the world we are living in; so let's take a look at what lights you up.

# Exercises

- What comes easy to you that is harder for others?
- If you got to do a month of fully paid work experience in any industry, job, business or hobby, what would you do?
- If you or your team had to apply your skills to something purely for the fun of it, what project would you like to work on?
- What did you discover about yourself when you answered these questions?

## Notes ...

## Curiosity overload

Most people hate junk mail. Most people hate opt-in websites and receiving email marketing. Most people hate trade shows and having people pitch to them. Most people hate being sold to, but then again, most people didn't build a multi-billion dollar business.

Kevin Harrington is the opposite. He loves hearing a great pitch, he enjoys catalogues, he devours emails, and he thrives at a trade show. He believes in something called, "curiosity overload." It's one of the principles he's built his fortune on.

When Kevin was twenty-three, he knew he wanted to be an entrepreneur, but he didn't know what business he would start. He decided to apply the principles of curiosity overload by attending every event he could, listening to every sales pitch he could and subscribing to as much marketing material that he could. He bombarded his brain with ideas and then he looked for the themes. He wasn't looking to copy someone else's thing; he was looking for his passion. He wanted to see what ideas would get him excited.

Kevin discovered something interesting; some of the ideas were easily forgotten, but some of them caused him to lose sleep a week later. Those were the ideas he wrote down in his book. After months of immersing himself in the world of products and business, he discovered some powerful ideas that were right for him.

Kevin went looking for a powerful combination – he wanted an exciting product, a person who could pitch it, statistics and reports that were impressive and a partnership deal that could get the product in front of a mass market. He cracked it for the first time when he discovered the Ginsu Knife being displayed at a trade fair and being pitched by humorous, old sales gun Arnold Morris. Kevin made a deal to get the man on TV from midnight to six a.m.

and ended up selling three million units of the product in under five years. Kevin's curiosity overload led to him creating the world's first infomercials and discovering hit product after hit product.

Kevin applied the formula and made a fortune selling cooking utensils, sporting equipment, music, franchises, computers and house wares. In front of the camera, he created dozens of Key People of Influence who could pitch and win sales of millions of dollars per week. Behind the camera, Kevin became an industry Key Person of Influence who attracted deals, products, endorsements and other opportunities that propelled him forward and allowed him to build a global business that made five billion dollars in sales.

Even as his success soared higher and higher, he made the conscious decision to stay curious and open. To this day, you'll see him reading blogs, watching crowd-funding videos, attending cutting-edge technology shows and judging venture capital pitching competitions, because he knows that curiosity and openness are a big key to his ongoing success.

How about you? Have you lost your curiosity or do you still have that spark from when you were a child? As a curious kid, you probably explored all sorts of ideas and discovered all sorts of things. As an adult, you may have learned to be more closed and shut off to new things.

As you read this book, your goal is to return to that youthful explorer you once loved to be. A lot of new ideas are coming your way, don't close them down. Allow a little bit of curiosity overload to ignite your flame. From a place of vitality, you'll do your best work.

## Vitality is more valuable than functionality

Key People of Influence are vital people, not functional people. You can't get the results you want without a vital person because they add something a functional person doesn't have. Functional people might be great at what they do, they might talk the talk and walk the walk, but at the end of the day, they are replaceable. If someone can find a cheaper option, they will take it because a functional person is just one possible solution to a problem.

A company can downsize functional people. A client can replace a functional supplier. An investor can put their money into something else that's just as functional. Functional does the job, but functional is still replaceable.

People who are in functional jobs see themselves as competent when executing a set of processes. They try to get better at those processes and they make marginal improvements. Functional people try to stay up to date with the standards and make sure they are able to perform as directed.

Functional people also worry. They worry about being downsized or overlooked for promotions. They are fearful that someone might come along who can do things better than they can. They are concerned about technology and new systems that could replace the tasks that they know how to complete.

Vital people see themselves as aligned to the result rather than the process. They don't care so much about *how* it happens. They ask questions about *why* we do things this way and *what* will it be like in the future. Vital people are worried about value. They want to deliver more of it, regardless of how it happens. No matter what, they will always be able to adapt and change dynamically if it gets them towards a better result, a faster result or a result that matters more.

The word *vital* has two potent definitions. One definition means "irreplaceable" and the other means "life-force." Vital people see themselves as being the "irreplaceable life-force" of a project, a business, an industry or even a cause. They feel like they own a specific piece of turf and that no one could replace them; any new people who show up are potentially new partners not competitors.

They see themselves as redefining the game in some way. They have opinions and their own unique take on things that makes them almost impossible to overlook.

Functional people are scared to take a holiday. They worry about what will happen while they are gone. Will they have a job to come back to? Will their clients find someone else? Will they lose opportunities they really need? A holiday is a scary thing to take when you are functional.

Vital people love taking holidays. They know that part of what makes them vital is that they have a certain spark that few people have and that they have fresh ideas that people want to tap into. For a vital person, a holiday is a place to get re-energized and to stimulate ideas. It's also a great reminder to everyone just how vital they are. A vital person knows that while they are gone, people are worried that they won't come back!

Functional people like to associate with people who reaffirm that life is tough. They like to be reassured that the economy is affecting others and that times aren't what they used to be. A functional person loves the comfort of their friends, who don't push them or inspire them to step up to a whole new level.

A vital person likes to be seen by their contemporaries. They welcome challenging debate and stimulating ideas. They want people to push them, to bring the best out of them and to stay true to the idea that there's always a new level to play at. A vital person will leave a group of people who slow them down for a group that stirs them up.

You can choose to become a functional person or a vital person. You can show up caring about the process or caring about the results. You can choose to take a stand for the way things are done or the way things could be done. You can be highly capable or highly irreplaceable.

A functional person wants to get more; a vital person wants to produce more.

A functional person wants to learn more; a vital person wants to share more.

A functional person wants to be shown a path; a vital person wants to create one.

A functional person is worn out by their functionality; a vital person is re-energized by their vitality.

The choice is yours from this moment forward; you can choose how you want to show up.

## Exercises

- Who do you know who shows up as a functional person?
- Who do you know who is currently a vital person?
- What are some of the differences you notice between them?

### Notes ...

## Your career is over

A career is "old technology." It was a great way to structure things at work for many years. It was an efficient way to get a return on the investment of training and developing staff.

That world is over. Today the world expects you to be trained, they expect you to educate yourself constantly and to bring something new to the table. For that reason, talented people move around.

The U.S. Department of Labor estimates that a worker who enters the labor force today will have ten to fourteen jobs by the time they are thirty-eight. In addition, top talent is increasingly mobile, living and working their way around the world.

It's easy to see where this trend is going. In the future we will see a massive trend towards "work on demand." Just like in Hollywood, teams come together to make a film project, they work together for six-to-twelve months and some of the people have multiple projects at once. At the end of the project, everyone goes their separate ways. They might work together again on another project or they might not.

Employers aren't dumb. They know that with increasingly strict labor laws, they can't run the risk of hiring people like they used to. They will outsource everything they can and only as a last resort will they hire people.

If you are already in business, don't think that you are safe either. With the speed at which things are moving today, your business is going to have to reinvent itself constantly. As an entrepreneur, almost every two years you're going to sit down and dream up a whole new plan for what you do and how you do it. If you don't, you'll be overtaken by those who do.

So if there's no security in jobs anymore, and if small businesses are constantly changing, where does someone go to create certainty and security for their income?

You go to your personal brand.

In the future your most valuable asset will be the number of people who know you, like you and trust you. In the future, you will be defined by your unique take on things, your story and your ability to innovate.

Every opportunity you get will involve a Google search of your personal brand. Every team you lead will be based on your story, not your resume. Every deal that makes you richer will complete because of who you are, not what it says on your business card.

In the future, you will discover that what you do might change, but your core passion only becomes stronger because everything you do reinforces a central theme.

From now on, you personally must see yourself as being in an enterprise that others need to know about. If you are in a job, your "enterprise" currently sells your time to your employer. More than that, it really sells a result that your employer wants.

If you are in business, you and your business need to become known for something unique as well. It's not enough to just offer a service at a fair price. You need to build a brand, develop your own intellectual property, accumulate stories and claim a leadership role within your niche.

You won't be known for the place that you work; you will be known for the people you're connected to, the ideas you are immersed in and what you care deeply about. Once these things are more widely known, you will have a constant stream of opportunities coming your way from places you've never been.

Your career may be dead, but if you position yourself as a Key Person of Influence, your adventure is just beginning.

## The harder you work, the less you earn

In the modern economy, hard work is not a competitive advantage anymore; everyone works hard. If you were to gather up all the hardest working people in the world, you would not find the top CEOs and the entrepreneurs, you would find the people who are struggling to make it up the ladder or struggling to survive at all. The competitive advantage is in thinking expansively, connecting with the right people and spotting fresh opportunities.

> *Your best ideas will come out to play...*
> *not to work.*

With that in mind, a week of sailing with friends could yield you more ideas, connections and perspective than a week of answering emails, catching up on paperwork and attending meetings. Attending a thought provoking conference could create more benefits in a day than months of repetitive tasks. As we discussed, the difference between the successful people on the planet is not functionality, it is vitality. Functionality is about performing a task well, whereas vitality is about doing it joyfully.

In the last ten years we have seen machines and systems replace a whole lot of functionality in the workplace; however, we are a long way from seeing the first machine that can compete with raw human vitality. Vitality yields creativity and innovation. It yields leadership. It yields boldness and robustness under pressure. It yields insights and breakthroughs. Software and machinery can't do that, software and machinery can only do the stuff that we call work.

If you look at the top earners, they don't consider what they do to be work. They are playing a game that they love and they make sure that it stays fun. They exude a level of vitality for what they do and because they love it, they get good at it.

The minute you begin to feel yourself working hard as opposed to playing a challenging game, it's time to take a break or get around some new people. Disappear for a week, get some sun, read up on your favorite role models, explore fresh ideas and spend time with people who are "in their zone." Attend a new event, read a new book and have a few new conversations.

More than anything, reconnect with your humanity. Beneath your desire to have a great home, a snappy wardrobe and some money in the bank is a part of you that longs to make a difference as well. Getting in touch with this part of you will give you a broadband connection to your vitality.

From a place of vitality, all the work comes easily, the ideas flow freely and the money comes in more effortlessly. An hour of inspiration is worth more than a week of drudging on. A day of play will do more for your career or business than a month of work. Success isn't about engaging in a struggle; it is about getting into the flow.

You can't expect things to change if you're not willing to get out of your comfort zone. You need to surround yourself with fresh ideas, insightful people and inspiring places. You need to be part of a peer group that holds you to a higher standard.

You owe it to yourself to stop working so hard and to start living your life in a way that lights you, and others, up.

# Exercises

Here are a couple of great questions you might want to explore:

- What would I love to do this week if I couldn't work?

- Who would I love to spend more time with who I don't normally see?

- Where would I love to be spending time this week if I wanted to be creative and adventurous?

- How would I love to deliver more value to others if I didn't need to worry about my schedule or my commitments?

- What difference would I love to make on the planet if I could just give my time and talent more freely?

## Notes ...

## Digital changed everything

The internet, mobile devices, software and automation have changed everything. New opportunities and challenges are emerging every day. Google allows people to answer almost every question that pops into their heads. Social media allows people to connect with like-minded individuals around the world. E-commerce allows anyone to sell products to a global marketplace. All the information is now connected, all the people are now connected and all the markets are now connected.

In the next ten years, we will see the effects of this and they will be huge. Until recently, the internet as we know it has been in development and people had been using it as a toy. Now people have integrated technology into the fabric of their being. It's hard to imagine a week without your smart phone, your wifi or your social networks. People are rapidly connecting the dots with all of this technology, and finding new and transformational ways to combine it all together.

One thing we know for sure is that whenever there is a new and more powerful way to connect and communicate, it has a huge impact on business. Phones, commercial air travel, television, email and mobile computing have all shown us that the companies that adapt quickly get a jump on those that don't.

When Kevin was growing his business, getting products from China meant going there, taking payments involved a team of people on phones, getting a product broadcast to an audience cost a fortune. It's now possible for a seventeen-year-old girl sitting in her bedroom to start a group on Facebook for free. She can have thousands of followers and fans worldwide for free. She can talk to them all on video for free. She can write to them all for free. She can get them all excited about her ideas... all for free.

This teenager can create or source a product easily and cheaply. She can design a brand easily and cheaply. She can have a web-store easily and cheaply. She can take payment easily and cheaply. She can send her products whizzing around the world easily and cheaply... all from her bedroom.

These are the times we live in. Already we are seeing people as young as twenty making six figure incomes from their "crazy" ideas. Most people think that these "whiz kids" are succeeding because they are good with technology, but this is not the reason.

These teenagers aren't stuck to the idea that a business has to be the way it used to be. They don't think a brand needs to cost a lot of money or that they need to live in a particular location in order to do business there. They don't think that their idea needs to please everyone or that they need to meet their clients face-to-face in order to deliver a powerful experience. That's why they are succeeding; not because they are better at using the technology, but because they are better at letting go of the way things were done in the past, probably because they were never attached to these ideas in the first place.

It's worth considering there is always a lag time between the release of new technology, its uptake and the real impact it has. Phones, radios, air travel, televisions, computers and email all took decades to reveal their full impact in the economy. Rest assured that social media, smart phones, crowd funding, 3D printing, wearable devices and cloud computing are all just getting warmed up and their full impact is still unknown.

As fast as the rate of change seems now, things are going to continue to speed up even more.

## The game has changed

The game has fundamentally changed. The internet, social media, mobiles, wearables, voice recognition, cheap processing power in everyone's pocket will change everything: every industry, every job, every business, every life on the planet. It's now possible to build a virtual business that owns little, but accomplishes a lot. You no longer need to buy phones, software, buildings or factories in order to make something. The most valuable components of a business today are the intangibles – the mission, the vision, the story, the brand, the intellectual property and the intelligent process that organizes people and things efficiently to get something done.

It's like when the combustion engine came along and the game changed. The Industrial Revolution introduced new technology that changed everything for people in the agricultural age. The people who used machines made fortunes and the people who stuck to their old ways ended up on the factory floor.

The economy is always looking for a better product at a lower price. For the last 150 years, big companies who have been able to afford big factories were the only ones able to deliver it. Not any more, not in this global, digital, connected economy.

New global small teams can also deliver high quality at a lower cost in many niches. Small teams can source products and ideas faster and more cheaply over the internet than big businesses can. The success of Uber and Airbnb has shown that owning an asset isn't required anymore. Being the person or company that coordinates a tribe of people is more valuable.

Small enterprise can access big factories when they need to, but don't have the overhead when they aren't using them. Smaller is lean but powerful in this economy. Small and lean is faster, more dynamic, cheaper and more flexible. Small is more fun. Small can look very big now. Best of all, small cares.

Small, lean enterprises give the feeling that they are making things for a special type of person rather than a market. Rather than buying things that everyone has, you can have unique things that were made for people *just like you*.

If you are a vegetarian and you want to go to the gym, you can learn from the world's best vegetarian bodybuilder. He could give you recipes, workout routines and products made just for vegetarian bodybuilders.

If you love 1960's vintage Mercedes-Benz convertibles, there is an online group you can join. There are blogs for people like you, and videos and downloads, and web stores to buy from. There will be a "hero" you admire, because she hates the same cars you hate just as much and she has a mint condition 1963 SL280.

If you love reading about deep sea free-diving, you can read the blogs from world champions. You can watch their HD home movies, listen to interviews with them, keep track of their adventures and even buy the same gear that they use.

On the internet, you are not some freak who is too fussy or who has strange taste. You are part of a "tribe," a gang of people who believe as you believe. This gang has conversations that "regular people" wouldn't understand. This gang has leaders. The Key People of Influence are the ones who lead these small, powerful teams. This gang has thousands and thousands and thousands of members who previously couldn't find each other but now they can.

Small, lean businesses have learned from big business and can now do what only big business could do up until recently. Now big organizations need to learn from small teams. Big organizations need to develop small, lean, dynamic teams within their large ranks. Big factories need to learn how to create things that are special and custom made. Big companies need to learn how to care deeply. Faceless corporations need to cultivate Key People of Influence to add personality to the big brand.

Whether you decide to start and grow your own business or develop a brand within a large organization, this is the most exciting time to be alive. Never has there been more meaningful work that needs to be done. Never has there been a better time to make a difference on the planet. Never has there been a better time to position yourself as a Key Person of Influence.

# Key Ideas

- The rules of the Industrial Revolution have changed.
- The world is now a deeply connected place and it requires a new type of leadership.
- People can find what they are looking for no matter where it is on the planet. They want it to be special, relevant and trustworthy.
- Traditional big business typically can't cater to these specific requirements of trust, character and uniqueness.
- Small highly niched businesses will emerge as profitable, fun places to be contributing.
- Every small niche will require a face to represent it. This will create the need for Key People of Influence in every niche in every industry.

## Notes ...

## The singer and the microphone problem

It's true that we live in a new and exciting time, thanks to technology. It's true that technology has changed everything. It's true that you need to get better at leveraging it. However, if you're going to be a Key Person of Influence, there's more to the story.

Imagine we live in 1876 and the first microphone has just been invented. It's an exciting new device that takes the human voice and amplifies it to a greater audience. This new technology is fascinating to a lot of people. Imagine there are seminars and courses on how to set up a microphone, how to switch it on, how to fiddle with the dials. Imagine people start writing articles like, "How To Make Millions With A Microphone," "Microphone Secrets" and "Microphone Wealth."

To some people it seems like the microphone is making people rich, but they are missing the point. The money doesn't go to people who know how a microphone works, it goes to the people who know how to sing. This presents a problem:

*A bad singer becomes a louder bad singer*
*with a microphone in their hand.*

Technology is really only valuable in the hands of someone who has a powerful message. Without a finely tuned human element, all the technology in the world isn't helpful.

Today, we have social media as the new "microphone." It takes a message and gets it out to the world almost instantly. Many people have become obsessed by this new technology. They attend courses called, "Social Media Millions," "E-Commerce Passive Income" and "Make Money Online." Some courses might be good, but many get people focused on the wrong thing. It's not social media, e-commerce platforms or a pretty webpage that makes people rich. It's their message.

Social media just makes people louder. The internet provides awesome leverage for a Key Person of Influence, but can be a waste of money someone else.

Just like a bad singer is a loud bad singer when they have a microphone, a boring business message gets ignored online and a terrible idea can haunt you for years.

If you were alive at the time of the microphone, I would advise you to get good at singing rather than setting up microphones. Today you need to get good at pitching your ideas, productizing your value, building your profile and partnering with other influential people. You don't need to get good at messing about with websites, apps, devices and other technology.

## Now is the time to be a Key Person of Influence

This book could not have been written any time in the past. Through the Middle Ages, you were either nobility or you were a serf. There was no chance to change things regardless of your passion or your talent.

As the Industrial Revolution was in full swing, there were also two types of people: those who could afford a factory and those who could not. A factory worker couldn't go out and start a rival business no matter how smart or hard working. There would be no point in telling people to go for their dreams; they simply didn't have any means of production to be vital; most people had to be functional or they would starve.

Today, all that has changed. Today, the "factory" costs almost nothing to set up (a laptop, a phone, a web site and a passion). And since the whole world can find you once you start taking your ideas online, every industry has broken down into sub-categories of niches within niches. I call these "micro-niches." Every industry you can imagine can be broken down into micro-niches and each one needs a Key Person of Influence.

Banking, telecommunications, energy, transportation, travel and mining – all of these big industries have been disrupted by people who went and set up a business within a micro-niche. Previously, they wouldn't have dared, now it happens every day.

In every niche and micro-niche there will be Key People of Influence. There is virtually a limitless demand for KPIs in the world right now. When someone asks, "Who's the best wedding make-up artist in Majorca?" you will be able to google them and find them easily. If someone wants to go on a holiday for Jewish singles, they can find the person who that does that. Crowd funding for startup entrepreneurs? Someone's leading it. A courier for stem cells? You'll find the person who's thought this through. Phone plans for ten year olds? There's a person who cares about this enough to find an innovative solution for parents.

In the next ten years there will be huge advantages for people who stand out as a Key Person of Influence in their chosen field. Teams will form around them, people will track them down from around the world, and the top money will flow to those who step up as a KPI in their industry. Fortunately you are at the beginning of a trend. Things are possible today that were not possible just a few years ago. You are a first settler in a brave new world.

## Niches and micro-niches are the new land

The British colonized Australia in the 1800s and many people became very rich by claiming their piece of land. The first settlers who staked their claim to a piece of land built their fortune by settling in one place and then working their land to produce as much as they could from it. People who failed to claim a piece of land wandered around aimlessly, doing odd jobs for the people who owned the land.

These itinerant workers, called swagmen, carried their rolled-up sleeping bags called "swags" on their backs as they navigated their way from farm to farm. They had no place to call home and they just kept wandering around looking for work wherever they could find it. After a while all the land was claimed and they were stuck feeling resentful that they hadn't staked their land when they had the chance. They complained that they worked hard and had to work too hard for every job.

In this new intangible economy the first settlers create wealth and power by staking their claim to a niche or a micro-niche. Mark Zuckerberg has claimed, "Social Networking." Sergey Brin and Larry Page claimed, "Search." Jeff Bezos claimed, "Online Shopping'". These are all examples of vast and fertile lands, but there's still plenty of territory for you to carve out your own space.

Owning a micro-niche is as valuable as owning land. If you are known as a Key Person of Influence in your field, you will attract the money and the opportunities that are flowing around that niche. Even when you pass opportunities to others, your wealth and power grows. The niche you claim is the place that people can easily find you. Others quickly figure out where you stand and send the opportunities your way.

Some people in the ideas economy aren't staking their claim to a niche or a micro-niche. They are the modern day swagmen who wander around looking at other people who have claimed their land. They keep coming up with new ideas, but aren't brave enough to settle on something and really give it a go. They want to try and please everyone, but they don't attract anyone.

After a while all the micro-niches in their industry will have Key People of Influence who have established themselves and these wandering swagmen will wish they had claimed their place sooner. They will resent the KPIs and say, "I could have done that," even though they didn't. Instead they become a wanderer who does odd jobs for Key People of Influence.

Do you want to be a swagman or a Key Person of Influence?

You can't have it both ways. You can't be a Key Person of Influence at "all sorts of things." You have to pick something that you are going to become known for and you need to start promoting it and turning away anything that isn't quite right. Even Mark Zuckerberg started with a micro-niche. He began by saying he had a social network that was only for Harvard students. Later he expanded Facebook a few micro-niches at a time before he claimed the whole territory.

Now is the time to claim your micro-niche too. It's the time to say:

> *"I won't try to be all things to all people. This is exactly what I do and this is my unique way of doing it. Anything else isn't for me."*

## Examples of niches and micro-niches:

### Niche: Heath and Wellness
Micro-niches: raw food parties, body-transformations for busy executives, fresh juice delivery, ten-day detox retreats, natural supplements in cakes, vegetarian marathons.

### Niche: Small Business Services
Micro-niches: hair salon marketing advice, Facebook advertising agency, testimonial video production in Manchester, alerts on distressed advertising space.

### Niche: House and Family
Micro-niches: news and advice for divorced fathers, dog furniture for Cocker Spaniels, accelerated learning for toddlers, portrait paintings of owners with their horses.

### Niche: Clothing and Apparel
Micro-niches: socks with motivational quotes, clothing that works with iPods, non-leather 'leather' jackets, fashion advice for CEOs of publicly traded companies.

### Niche: Travel
Micro-niches: LGBT travel, cruises for people over age sixty-five, trips that follow the F1 circuit for a year, diving trips to rebuild a reef.

## Every industry will be finely sliced
In every industry there are going to be micro-niches within the niches. Each micro-niche will be an opportunity for a Key Person of Influence to claim it as their space. The internet will allow people

from all over the world to find that Key Person of Influence and do business with them. People who fail to claim a micro-niche will wish they had because the internet doesn't really help generalists to stand out.

## It can make sense to limit your clientele

There are two common ways to think about your customer base: it can be either wide or it can be tall. Wide means that you have many customers who all make small purchases. Think about snack companies—they sell millions of candy bars to millions of people, each of whom buy a few. It's a very wide customer base. Tall, on the other hand, means that you have strong relationships with a small number of customers. Think about a consulting firm that only has half-a-dozen clients or the manufacturers of heavy industrial equipment. Each customer counts for a lot.

Either strategy can work, depending on your market and your product. Automobile companies are one example; some make huge numbers of cheap, affordable cars that are meant to be sold to millions. Others specialize in expensive, handmade vehicles that have a much smaller market where each customer is worth much more.

There's a lesson to be learned here, and it goes against some conventional marketing wisdom. Namely this,

> *"You always want as many*
> *customers as possible."*

Sure, if you're going wide, then you do want as many customers as possible. And in the twentieth century – the golden age of mass production – going wide was the name of the game. This is the basic assumption many people have about the nature of marketing.

But we don't live in the twentieth century any more. It doesn't always make sense to go as wide as possible with your customer base. In fact, and especially for entrepreneurs, it usually doesn't. Can you compete with the Wal-Mart of your industry? Probably not, if you're relatively small. Instead, you need to exploit the weakness of the big business with the wide customer base.

People are all different, but a mass-produced product is made to try and satisfy everyone. That means an inevitable dumbing-down of whatever the product is. That's your opening.

Your starting point is to find a group of people who are dissatisfied with the current offering (it's easy, now that we have the internet). Figure out a way to give them what they need and forget about everyone else for now. Focus your efforts like a laser beam on that micro-niche, become the KPI in that space and you'll soon be able to charge a premium for your products and services as you look after people better than they've ever experienced.

A tall customer base is valuable and that's where growth lies in today's market. With this model, it's okay to have a small number of customers who you really look after. Instead, focus on deepening your relationships with them, finding new ways to create value, and building new systems to generate revenue from your existing client base. You'll be able to afford to specialize in ways that larger companies can't, and that's where you'll have the advantage.

You don't always have to get as many customers as possible. Go micro-niche instead of mass market, and you'll open up all sorts of new opportunities that aren't available to everyone else.

# Exercises

- Make a list of micro-niches in the industry you most enjoy (Think: gender, geography, specialty, common interest).

- Google some of these micro-niches to see if someone has already claimed this land or if it's still available for you to own (soon we will discuss how).

Imagine if there was one specific thing you would love to be known for, what would it be?

## Notes ...

## You already have a unique set of skills and talents

The good news is, in these exciting times, almost anything can be turned into a fun, profitable business. Your greatest asset is your existing passion, the skills you already have and, most of all, your own personal story. You may think that the key to your wealth lies in some mystical wealth creation vehicle that you don't yet know about. Maybe you think it's the Stock Market or property development or a franchise or a multi-level-marketing company.

The truth is that your real wealth lies in your story. Your journey thus far has not been a waste of time; it's been perfect. Your hobbies and interests are not meaningless, they are a gold mine. Your passion isn't hollow; it's the best fuel you will ever have.

Jack Lalanne was a retired fitness trainer who looked amazing for his age and had the agility of a man twenty years his junior. Kevin discovered his secret was freshly made juices. They worked with his existing insights and came up with the "Power Juicer," that product has exceeded one billion dollars in sales globally!

Jack's wealth didn't come from discovering something in another industry, it came from exploring his story and the insights he took for granted.

You've already been a leader within certain circles. You already have examples of people you've helped, teams you've built and value you've added. You need to harness what you have and refine it.

Quite literally, there are already people taking home six-figure incomes from their passion for the strangest things. Right now there are people making great money from:

- Teaching people to do their make-up to look like comic book characters.

- Assembling flat packed furniture for people who like IKEA products, but hate using an Allen Wrench.

- Giving advice on setting up a branch of your business in Singapore.

- Running yacht races in Thailand.

- Selling fake diamonds that stick to your groin.

- Helping professional speakers fine tune the last ten minutes of their talk.

- Sourcing investment properties for young professionals who work for the major banks or consulting firms.

- Selling special bags of organic mixed fruit and nuts that replace all meals for a week.

- Helping millionaires learn how to captain their new boats.

- Helping people eat the same diet as our Paleolithic ancestors.

But here's the problem; every day you will open the paper and read about someone who has made big money doing some new thing. You hear a story about some newly made millionaire who is achieving success in some strange and different industry.

The assumption you may wrongly make is that it was the "thing" that made the money. You might think it was the product or the industry that was responsible for their success and miss that it was in fact the marriage of that "thing" with that person's story.

You may curse yourself for missing out on the latest trends:

"Oh, if only I was in the property flipping game."

"I wish I had developed that iPhone App."

"Of course, it's currency trading I should be doing."

"Why didn't I think of being a life-coach sooner?"

"What was I thinking by not being part of that franchise last year?"

"I knew I should have been part of that MLM from the start."

It all looks very attractive when you see someone succeeding

## ... *But* their *thing might not be* your *thing.*

What you may miss altogether is the story behind the story.

The person who just made a fortune from sourcing real estate loved looking for real estate deals for a long time before they got rich doing it.

The person who trades the markets was happy riding through the ups and downs for a long time before they had their payoff.

The life coach did three years of unpaid work in the industry before they got their first client and another seven before they became the highly paid speaker you saw on stage.

The guy with the organic fruit and nuts business has been writing about health and wellness issues since he was sixteen years old.

It's their story that people buy into. You like them. You like their take on things. You like their ideas. You see how connected they are in their industry. You want to spend time and money with them because they are a Key Person of Influence and that's attractive to you.

The person in the story hasn't found *the* thing, they have found *their* thing. However, I could almost guarantee that it's not *your* thing. Unless you have been keenly interested in something for at least seven years, forget trying to be a success story in that field any time soon. You simply can't outdo the people who genuinely love that industry, not because they think it is a quick formula for cashing in.

But wait a minute. Aren't we contradicting what was said earlier? Didn't it say earlier in this book that it takes just twelve months to become a Key Person of Influence? Now I'm saying seven years! No, I said...

> *"How to become one of the most highly valued and highly paid people in the industry you love."*

The most important words in that sentence are "in the industry you love." You already have a story; you already have a set of skills, talents and experiences that are valuable. It's time to see your story for what it's really worth.

There is already a theme to your life that has been unfolding. It may seem that you have done many things or that you have some strange and unrelated talents, but it hasn't been random at all. Everything you have done up until this point has been for a specific reason. It has brought you right here to this chapter in this book where you can get this message.

*"You are already standing on a mountain of value. Your story is valuable, your experience is unique, and you are highly valuable... just as you are!"*

You don't need to learn new skills; you are ready to create value now. You are no longer on this planet to be a consumer; you are here to be a producer. You're ready to establish yourself as a Key Person of Influence through creative output not through further consumption. All of your future learning will come from the process of producing value not through pursuing other people's story or distant trends.

This may rattle you a little. Surely, if you were valuable already you would already be earning the serious money? No, the reason you don't have the money yet is that you have not established yourself as a KPI and you haven't crystallized your value into products. In the next few chapters you will see exactly how to do this in five clear steps.

When you are ready, let's take a look at the Key Person of Influence Method.

# Exercises

- Map out the timeline of your life with high points and low points. Start out as early as you can remember and try to remember some of the details for each memory.
- Once you have your life's timeline, look for the themes.
- Make a list of your skills and talents and see if you can join them up into a micro-niche.

## Activity

On your bathroom mirror stick a sign that reads:

"I am already standing on a mountain of value. My story is valuable, my experience is unique, and I am highly valuable as I am. All of my future learning will come from the process of creative output."

# Notes ...

# ②

# THE KEY PERSON OF INFLUENCE METHOD

*KPI traditionally refers to a "Key Performance Indicator" – a benchmark that people measure themselves against. Likewise, a Key Person of Influence sets a standard that others aspire to. If you become a Key Person of Influence, people will associate you with the level of performance they want to align with.*

*It's time for you to become a KPI.*

## Stepping into the inner circle

In every industry there's an inner circle of Key People of Influence. If there's a good opportunity in their industry, these people are the first to be told. If they don't like the opportunity, they pass it to another KPI. If all the KPIs don't like the opportunity, they kick it out to the outer circle.

This sets up an interesting situation. The inner circle is rich with good opportunities shared between a small number of people. The outer circle is full of many people fighting over the poor opportunities. For this reason...

> *"... Until you are a Key Person of Influence in the industry you love, your full-time job is to become one."*
> #kpibook

Nothing could illustrate this point more than the income inequality in the USA, supposedly a country where anyone can get ahead if they have a dream, work hard and act smart. The top ten percent of the USA's wealthy control about eighty percent of all the wealth. The top one percent control about a third!

What does this tell you about how money works across the whole of the USA? It tells you that it's not even close to being "fairly" distributed. Wealth moves to and from a small percentage of *Key People of influence.*

If you are in the top ten percent, you can expect to be sharing in eighty percent of the wealth. If you aren't, you will be fighting it out with the other ninety percent of people for the remaining twenty percent of the wealth – it will be exhausting and dehumanizing.

It works in much the same way inside your industry. The top twenty percent of companies in any industry often generate more than eighty percent of the revenue in that industry. The top ten percent of people who run those top companies are earning fortunes, while the majority of people are trying to budget their pay each month.

If you've heard about people taking an exponential leap in their earnings, let's shine some light on why. If a person moves from the average in their industry into the top third of earners, they won't actually see a big shift in their income or their influence. They won't really get any special treatment, they won't hear about fresh opportunities and they won't stand out significantly in their industry even though they moved from the mid-point to the top third.

If that same person moves into the top ten percent of their industry, their life changes dramatically. As soon as a person crosses over to being on the inner circle of their industry, they start sharing ninety percent of the pie with their new contemporaries.

This book isn't about the philosophical arguments of whether this is right or wrong. It's about doing the things that get you into the top ranks as fast as you can. One of the best ways to redistribute wealth is to get more people using the skills and strengths of successful entrepreneurs and leaders.

As you progress deeper into the inner circle and establish yourself as a Key Person of Influence, your income takes a leap, you get invited into important meetings, your voice gets heard and you have more input. It becomes a virtuous loop, the more input, the more you are seen as valuable and the more you get known as a Key Person of Influence in your field.

You must orchestrate your move into the inner circle of the industry you love. It's the most rewarding thing you can do. There's very little happening outside the inner circle that's worthy of your time.

## How are you showing up?

Both Kevin and I have been invited as speakers at events around the world. At these events, celebrity speakers and expert presenters are regularly paid more money in a day than many people earn in a year. These events pull in crowds of people who want to learn from the top speakers. Before the events even start, I can see how people kept themselves in the bottom ninety percent without knowing it. I also see firsthand how some people make small shifts and find themselves in the top one percent of earners in their industry in under twelve months.

Let me explain.

Kevin and I have each seen well over 100,000 people networking at conferences and business events. If you watch closely you'll see why some people succeed and some people fail. Most people are abysmal at generating any attraction from others. Most people walk away from a business event with nothing more than a small stack of business cards from people who have no interest in doing any business with them. Most people get excited when they add someone on LinkedIn, even though that person is just being polite. It's crazy that these people are at an event with hundreds of motivated, screened people and yet somehow they can't do any business as a result of being there.

It's not because they are bad people or that they don't have any value to share. It's simply that they have never been taught how to

represent themselves as a Key Person of Influence. They are often unclear about the value they can offer, they seem to lack credibility that others can gauge, they come across as burned-out, lacking enthusiasm or unwilling to do anything to win business.

A Key Person of Influence doesn't show up that way. They are clear, credible, energized and they don't seem needy. They have the groundwork in place so they can show up confidently.

It doesn't take long to see the difference. At almost every event I've ever spoken at, someone comes up and asks about doing a deal of some sort with me. At this point, I don't care if the person is a trained speaker or if they have a well-conceived deal in mind. First, they need to know if they are a Key Person of Influence.

I ask some typical questions (some I ask directly and some I'm mentally checking for):

## Question One: What do you do?

It seems like a very open and general question, but I actually want to know that they stand out purely on how they pitch themselves at that point.

Most people say their job title or profession, "I'm a management consultant," "I'm a dentist," "I run a car dealership," "I'm in recruitment." Some attempt to be unique and say something like, "I motivate people to be their best," or something vague like "I help people get what they want," or general along the lines of "I help businesses grow."

A KPI lights up when you ask them what they do. They are prepared and they already know you'll be blown away before they have opened their mouth. In under two minutes, they have you hooked. Their response has been honed and it's powerful. They speak clearly, with authority and relevance. They often can communicate more in two minutes than others can in an hour.

## Question Two: What makes you credible?

I might ask, "Do you have a book? Do you have a following? Are you published in any journals or magazines? Do you have any remarkable case studies? Do you have any unique insights that few people can articulate?"

If I do ask, most people fumble and feel awkward that they have no proof of their value. They say, "I've been doing this for fourteen years," or "I have some good testimonials."

A KPI will ooze credibility. They will tell you about their insights, their thought leadership and the publications they are featured in. They will talk about their case studies and success stories and within seconds you know they are a legitimate professional in their field.

## Question Three: How do you make your money?

"Do you sell your time? Do you have products? Do you broker someone else's products and services? What do people usually pay you and are they typically happy with it?"

Most of the time their "product" is them. They need to physically turn up in order to deliver value. Conversely, they may have a product that is generic that I instantly compare it to other products in the market and I can't see what's special about their offering.

A Key Person of Influence has an elegant business model backing them up. They have an ecosystem of products and services that all fit nicely with their brand. They know how to differentiate their products just by the way they describe them.

## Question Four: I ask,

"Is this person known, liked and trusted within their industry?"

"If I google your name, what will I find? Will videos of you come up on YouTube? Will I see that you have thousands of Twitter followers? Will I find anything offensive? Will I find anything about you at all?"

Most people don't have a profile even when you google their name. If you're lucky you'll get their LinkedIn and Twitter accounts. Rarely will you see blogs, videos, audios and community pages. It's even more unlikely to find feature articles about them from external sources, reviews or interviews. Many people want someone else to build their profile or expect they will get a profile after a deal comes off. The problem is that deals won't even get started if a person is an unknown commodity.

A KPI shows up when you google them. They have several coherent social media profiles. You'll find engaging video and audio, you'll see them written up in traditional media and you'll see their work reviewed by third parties.

## Question Five: What else can you bring to the deal?

Do you bring with you access to new products, big brands, wide reaching distribution, celebrities, skilled team members, databases or money? Do you know how to structure a deal? Do you think win/win?

Often people will communicate inadvertently that they want the whole deal to be easy for them and difficult for me. They want to show up and speak, have my company promote their products or for me to buy what they have to sell without asking too many questions.

When a KPI approaches me, doing a deal is easy and their approach is win/win. They volunteer the additional benefits they bring to the deal. They have already thought about how the deal might be structured so it's almost risk free. They make sure they take on an equal share of the burden to execute the deal because they know how much work is actually involved in getting anything meaningful achieved.

Within minutes, I know the difference between a Key Person of Influence and someone who's not there yet. It doesn't take long to make a deal or to pass on an opportunity because I know the KPI is prepared.

In the next chapters, I'm going to outline a specific five-step method for you to follow. It's designed so that you are seen to be a Key Person of Influence in your industry. It builds in clarity, credibility, scale, transparency and commercial viability. It's designed to leverage your story, your experiences, your insights and your personality.

When you're ready to learn and apply this method, read on.

# THE KEY PERSON OF INFLUENCE METHOD

As we just discussed, across all industries, the top opportunities go directly to a small group of people who present themselves as a Key Person of Influence in that field. The rest of the people in the industry are left to fight over the opportunities that the KPIs turn down. It might sound a bit unfair but that's how it is.

It's not that hard to become a Key Person of Influence and it certainly doesn't take years to achieve. There are five things that you need to have in place for you to demonstrate that you are a Key Person of Influence:

## 1. Pitch: Your ability to communicate your value and uniqueness through your spoken word.

Key People of Influence can answer the question, *"What do you do?"* with power and clarity.

Powerful pitching is the ability to clearly communicate your message in a way that encourages people to support and contribute to your projects.

Pitching is a vitally important skill. If you have something of great value to offer, but no one can understand it, you're not going any further. Throughout history every great business, movement or cause began with a powerful pitch. Armed with little more than their words, many people throughout history have launched a business, recruited a team, gained funding and even changed the world. In fact, many people who've had resources couldn't get things done when the pitch was lousy.

Key People of Influence pitch for specifics. They don't cast a wide net, they are laser focused. When you have a great pitch you don't just make more money and attract great people, you also have more fun, attract further opportunities and experience deeper rewards.

## 2. Publish: Your ability to gain credibility through authoring content.

Published content creates ownership and authority over your chosen niche or micro-niche. If we were in the agricultural age you'd need the "Title Deed" to your land. In a global market full of ideas, published content online shows ownership, it puts your name on your work. Published books, blogs, articles and reports tell the world that you are an authority in your field. It's no coincidence that the word "authority" has the word "author" in it.

These days you can publish short runs of books, you can instantly upload blogs, it's inexpensive to make beautifully designed reports and it's almost effortless to make it all available globally. If you publish, your ideas get seen and they spread faster.

The process of writing will make you smarter than most in your field, it will sharpen your stance on each topic and help you to spot trends in your thinking. Published content on its own is an intellectual property asset that can be further developed in your products.

## 3. Product: Your ability to scale your value through an elegant product and services ecosystem.

Turning your skill set into an asset is an essential part of becoming a Key Person of Influence and this happens when you productize your intellectual property. The products you represent will play a central role in the commercial success of your enterprise.

You must have several products each designed to complement the overall mission you have as a Key Person of Influence. Part of that challenge is to have products that are built for high volume and some that are built for high value.

Products help you to become known and transfer value. Even services businesses can create a "productized service" and develop additional products that complement the core services business. As soon as you develop quality products you'll increase your opportunities to grow or even go global if you want to.

### 4. Profile: Your ability to become known, liked and trusted in your industry.

When people do a search for your name, you must come up on the first results page that you are clearly a Key Person of Influence in your chosen field. There is no longer an excuse for being invisible online. You are who Google says you are. If you're invisible, you won't complete bigger deals no matter how good you pitch.

You're in control of your online profile. It's your responsibility to create a powerful online presence using social media and traditional media hand in hand. It's important to clean up anything that's confusing or outdated and to remove anything that doesn't serve your personal brand. With a well-crafted profile you'll discover perfect inbound opportunities start to show up regularly and you get more success with what you go after.

### 5. Partnership: The ability to structure and maintain strategic relationships that benefit everyone involved.

Like you might have guessed, the real wealth comes when you complete this final stage and begin leveraging with others in an effective way. The spirit of partnership generates a multiplier effect. Rather than two people competing over how to slice a pie, they work together to build a bakery and produce more pies than they know what to do with.

Consider that there is already someone who has a list of thousands of potential customers for your product. There are already experts in your industry who would jump at the chance to be interviewed by you to create a product that enhances their brand and yours. There are already people who have products that your contacts would be interested in and they would happily pay you a healthy percentage for making the sale.

## The order is important

There's no point trying to skip over any of the five steps. You can't just leap straight into a lucrative partnership if you have a poor pitch, no credibility, a broken business model and you're invisible in your industry. If you try to create a product but you can't pitch it, it's not going to find its market. Building a profile without any written content just doesn't work.

Real money can be made from partnerships but they don't happen until people know that you are a KPI. The fastest way to become a KPI in your industry is by doing these five steps in the order they've been given to you (Pitch, Publish, Productize, Profile and Partnerships).

## Then the results come

When you have all five steps in place, you will be amazed at what happens to your life. You will be asked to speak at events, you will be referred to as an "expert," you will get more focused opportunities coming your way, you will be able to access most people in your industry and you will earn more money with less struggle.

This method has transformed people's lives and businesses in over fifty different industries in a dozen different countries. If you implement this method, it will transform your business and your life, too. You will become a person of vitality rather than a person of functionality.

These five strengths are the cornerstones of hyper-resourceful people. This isn't voodoo; it's best-practices that you can see working in the real world.

Becoming a KPI is not about late nights sweating over text books, getting more qualifications, or putting in another few year's hard slog in the office. The faster you can get these five steps completed with high standards, the faster you will be a Key Person of Influence on the inner circle of the industry you love.

Sadly, you get no points for trying to complete these steps. You only see big results after all five steps are completed with high standards. Almost having a book means you have zero books on Amazon. Almost having a product means you have nothing to sell but your time. Almost doing a partnership means you are still working alone.

For some time you'll be putting in the effort and the results won't appear because the five steps aren't yet complete. Stay with it. Keep going. It will be worth it when you've completed all the steps. Influence comes from output, not from hard work.

In the next chapters we will examine ways to get a breakthrough in each of the five steps of the KPI Method.

## Key Person of Influence Scorecard

Before you read on, take the Key Person of Influence Quiz at: *www.keypersonofinfluence.com/scorecard*

This is a set of questions designed to score you on the five areas of influence described in this book. It gives you a customized report based on your answers. The results of this quiz will give you a starting point and show you where you are already strong and where you need to focus your attention.

IF SOMEONE GOOGLED YOUR NAME, WOULD THEY FIND MOST OF PAGE 1 IS POSITIVE LINKS FEATURING YOU?

# YES NO

# STEP ONE: PITCH

Your pitch is so much more than you may think. The truth is, with a perfect pitch you will be swamped with opportunities.

On the hit show *Shark Tank* people get onto the show because of their pitch. They then get investment, distribution and endorsement because of their pitch. The Sharks make their decision to bite based upon the quality of the words and the strength of the delivery in the pitch. Consider that many of the greatest wealth creators and change-makers throughout history started with little more than a persuasive pitch.

Here are some excerpts from pitches that changed the world:

*"I have a dream that someday this nation will live up to its creed that all men are created equal."*
Dr. Martin Luther King Jr.

*"We choose to go to the moon by the end of this decade, not because it's easy but because it's hard."*
John Fitzgerald Kennedy

*"You must be the change you want to see in the world."*
Mahatma Gandhi

*"Let's measure the success corporations by how much they enhance human well-being."*
Anita Roddick

Can you imagine asking these visionaries, "What do you do?"

Their response would be so exhilarating, provocative and contagious that you would want to help them in any way you could. That is how you want people to react to your ideas.

I often ask business people to rate themselves on how well they think they answer the question, "What do you do?" Most give themselves seven or eight out of ten, but is this realistic?

Consider that everyone you meet knows over 250 people. A ten out of ten would mean they want to tell everyone about you. They would want to phone their most prized contacts and introduce you. A ten out of ten means that people will openly share their time, contacts and resources with you.

With this in mind, most people rate one to two out of ten at best. They leave over eighty percent of potential on the table in every single interaction.

Don't be discouraged; get excited. There is massive room to grow just by improving the way you describe what you are up to in the world. When someone asks you the quintessential networking question "What do you do?," your enthralling answer will have the power to unlock all of their resources. A not-so-potent answer will elicit a polite response, but nothing much will come of the interaction.

## Crafting the perfect pitch changes everything

In baseball terminology, a perfect pitch often results in a strikeout. But when it comes to the perfect pitch made by an entrepreneur looking to launch a product or company – well, that perfect pitch often results in a home run.

In more than two decades of work as an investor and entrepreneur – a period when Kevin Harrington launched more than 500 products with cumulative sales of more than $5 billion worldwide – he's heard countless pitches. Sadly, the majority of these pitches were far from perfect. Kevin's company usually gets over 1,000 submissions a month. His staff then whittle the number down to about 100 "maybes." Ultimately, only two or three of those products get launched every month.

You only get one chance to make a good first impression. Don't approach this moment ill-prepared.

Pitching an idea to single customer or a group of strangers can be intimidating. But at that moment, all you have to do is talk about a product or service you believe in – and do it in a passionate, authoritative and thoroughly researched manner. Prepare yourself by doing your pitch in front of a camera or a mirror. Do your presentation for your spouse or your kids. Practice. Don't ever go into a pitch situation cold.

If you've not had much success with previous pitches, it's time to change it up – and fast! If you do what you've always done, you'll get what you've always gotten. You can't just sit and do it the way you've always done it.

The "Snuggie" is a good example from Kevin's many successful product launches. If somebody walked into his office and said, "I have invented a blanket with arms and it's is going to do $400 million in sales," Kevin would have asked them what they'd been drinking before asking them to leave his office.

But they didn't approach it that way, instead they worked their pitch to perfection and they ended up with a deal. They then worked their on-air pitch hard until it was a top performer. When it came time to go into retail stores, they didn't let knockoffs come in because their pitch to retailers was also very powerful. When they went to the buyers, they pitched them by saying, "We're going to give you the original, but if you sell other brands, we can take our brand out of your store." By pitching the deal well to investors, then on TV and then to the retailers, they've sold more than twenty million units and kept copy-cats at bay. The entrepreneurs behind Snuggie discovered that the quality of their business comes down to the quality of their pitch.

## Get help with your pitch

If you're having trouble getting your pitch off the ground, go to people who have been there before and seek advice on what they've done. Get mentors who can advise you. Both Kevin and I utilize people outside our company who have a fresh perspective and past experience building businesses.

Don't be afraid to pick up the phone to have someone help you work through the weaknesses of your pitch. In the beginning, you have to get out there and pitch to people who can help you develop your business approach.

Sometimes you have to reboot or hit the reset button and start over when creating a pitch. Eventually you will hit the point where you believe in yourself and your pitch. Then it's time to see how others respond.

## Beware of the polite response

A polite comment is one of the worst responses you can get when you tell people what you do. It is polite responses that keep you looking good, but going nowhere. You can go nowhere for years because of polite responses.

Most people think it is encouraging that others nod and smile. When someone says, "Sounds interesting" or "How long have you been doing that?" it is actually a meaningless non-response. They are being polite, but in truth are not engaged or interested. What you want is an emotionally-charged response. They should either love it or hate it. Ideally, you want to see some immediate action.

You want people to engage with you. They should either want to pull out their calendar and make a time to talk to you, open their contacts and put you in touch with someone they know or tell you, "Your idea will never work!"

Positive or negative, a strong reaction is much better than a polite, benign response because you know they are listening and considering your ideas, not dismissing you. You must stir up a reaction and make a connection. Be anything but boring.

## Speaking with power

It isn't just for one-to-one interactions that your pitch comes out to play. The day you get invited to speak in front of a group or to the media is the day your life can change dramatically. I have seen great speakers take the stage, share their vision and rally incredible amounts of support. I have seen a forty-five minute talk raise millions. I have seen an eight minute pitch that resulted in over 250 people rushing to grab a business card from the presenter (it held up the event by over thirty minutes). I've watched eighteen minute talks that have changed my outlook on life.

When you know where you stand and what you stand for you become a magnet for opportunity. When you can communicate that message to a group, you speed up time and can achieve a month's work in a day. People see your vision, they see you leading the way, and they come rushing at you with every resource you could ever need, want or imagine.

But who are you to command that attention? Who are you to have people rushing your way? What's so special about you? Let's find out.

## You are already standing on a mountain of value

Remember, your story is already more valuable than you think. Don't dare throw out your history. Sometimes it is simply that it is difficult to see your own value and you need to speak with others about your ideas and dreams.

Where I grew up in Queensland, Australia there is an ancient ridge of volcanic mountains called the Glass House Mountains. We would climb the imposing giant, Mount Tibrogargan. From the summit, you get a view of how massive all the other smaller mountains are and it doesn't feel like you are standing on the tallest mountain of the group. From that lofty vantage point, the peaks are equalized.

Most people are already standing on a mountain of value; however, it is difficult to see the size, shape and attributes of the mountain when you are on it. When you look down, all you see is the dirt beneath your feet, and when you look up, you see how impressive the other mountains are.

It is very easy to see value from a distance. You see the value in others so effortlessly, but you sometimes fail to notice the immense value in yourself.

This is why you need to engage with some trusted friends, and even some objective people you don't know, to get their input. You need to get someone else to reflect back to you what they see as your value and how it should be packaged. We've run pitching workshops all over the world and seen that an experienced entrepreneur with some perspective can often tell you more about the value you offer than your closest friend or spouse.

Get yourself around a dynamic person who can take you through a process of questioning and making suggestions until you have a pitch that you feel proud of. People who have worked with our team discover that their story is already of amazing value when pitched correctly. One of the most exhilarating things I get to witness on a regular basis is when someone breaks through and sees how much they have to offer the world just as they are.

Sometimes it is overwhelming to people when they see what they have been hiding. It's like discovering you have an original Van Gogh sitting in your basement! Many people unlock a burst of energy they never knew they had.

## Discover your Big Game

Throughout your career as a leader or entrepreneur you'll be required to pitch constantly. You'll pitch for investment, for distribution, for deals, for top employees to join your team, for sales and sometimes for forgiveness when you make a mistake. The common element that sits beneath every pitch is the "Big Game" you're playing for; the reason why you're doing all of this stuff.

Your pitch must contain your *why*. It's your compass. It's the reason you get up each day.

Bill Gates said Microsoft's Big Game was "to put a Personal Computer in every home and on every desk in the world."

Ray Kroc said that McDonald's Big Game was, "If Man goes to the moon, we will go there too, open a restaurant and serve him a great burger at a great price."

Oprah Winfrey said her Big Game was "to share a daily

dose of inspiration with women all over the world."

My Big Game is to "create influential leaders and entrepreneurs all over the world who have the resources to solve manful problems at scale."

**Your Big Game should:**

- Get you out of bed raring to go in the morning and keep you up late at night.
- Become the heart of how you design your business and how you get results.
- Become the source of the irresistibly delightful experience you deliver to everyone who comes into contact with you.

Your pitch is not just a set of well-rehearsed words. It is a statement about what you are up to in the world. It's your Big Game that lights you up just thinking about it.

## Here are the components to create a game worth playing:

**It must be fun:** There is no point playing a game that is no fun. Sure, it will have its share of struggles. It will have its frustrations and at times it may seem impossible. Underneath the challenges, it will still be an exciting and fun game you want to get up each day and play.

**It must have rules:** There are clear structures, time frames and behavior that is out of bounds You must be able to explain to people the rules of the game. Someone on your team might ask, "Why do we spend so much time with customers after they already buy from us?," to which you might say, "One of the rules of the game is that we must have customers who feel respected and appreciated by us and rate us at least eight out of ten on customer service."

**There must be players:** Every game has players who come to the game because they consider their strengths well suited to the game. The better your players, the more fun the game. It's fun to watch the NBA because all the players are almost super human. Your game should be set up in a way that attracts top players want to join you to demonstrate their abilities.

**There must be a prize:** Committed players love to play for the fun of the game, but when you have a coveted prize at stake, everything goes to the next level. Is it money? Is it ownership? Is it recognition? Is it something even bigger? Whatever it is, the prize must be exciting for the players.

**There must be a way to win:** Imagine a game that has no end time. Imagine a game that doesn't keep score. Imagine a game where there is no clear way to win. It would not be fun and it would not keep people interested.

As the inventor of your game, you get to set the goal posts that let you know when you are winning and how you will know when you have won. Just like professional sporting events, your game should offer short-term wins as well as an overall championship victory.

The thought of winning should stir you up emotionally and make you feel a surge of energy and focus.

**There must be a way to lose:** If you can't lose the game, then it's no fun either. The game must be edgy enough that the players realize it's entirely possible to lose. The thought of losing the game should be a strong driver, and there should be a point where it is clear the game has been lost so players know when it's time to go back to the locker room and rethink their strategy.

The question you must ponder again and again is this:

> *"What's the Big Game I would love to play over the next three years... Win or Lose?"*

The answer needs to make you feel enlivened. When you have that answer you are ready to construct your pitch around your Big Game.

# Exercises

- Write the words "My Big Game" in the center of a piece of paper and mind map the factors that are important to you.

- Make sure you have insights for each of the above six components in your Big Game.

## Notes ...

## You can't please everyone

The next point to start with is to choose specific micro-niche, a place that you can start your Big Game from.

As we discussed, even a massive phenomenon like Facebook started out exclusively for Harvard University students to share their drunken photos. They then expanded to allow all university students, then piece by piece they conquered the internet. From a tiny micro-niche, big things can grow, but it almost never happens that a business sets out to please everyone and actually achieves it.

You need to consider your industry niche carefully and then add more criteria. You need to know exactly who you are you trying to serve.

Is your business going to specialize in a gender, an age group, a geographic location, an ideology or a socio-economic group?

Will you focus on a specific need, common beliefs and values, or a common frustration or problem of a specific group?

More often than not, *you* will be the micro-niche. Your target market comprising a specific age group and gender will be you. The frustrations will be yours (either past or present). If you can relate to these issues personally, you can craft something that fits your niche. Alternatively you might target a niche based on your past because you can remember vividly a struggle that needs addressing.

Your micro-niche should consist of people who you would enjoy connecting with and people who would equally enjoy connecting with you. If you are not a vegetarian, don't make it part of your niche just because you think it makes business sense. You will either get found out as a hypocritical meat-eater, or you will end up hating your business because it's not a good fit with who you are. Choose a micro-niche that you identify with personally, with genuine concern and interest. Say "no" to other opportunities until you've achieved notoriety within a micro-niche.

## Use a sniper rifle, not a shotgun

Intuitively, people believe that taking a general, encompassing approach to pitching is more effective than a narrowly focused pitch; experience shows me it is not. When you try to catch everyone in your net, you catch no one. The "cast your net wide" approach to business is well and truly dead. A broad approach is especially ineffective when you are starting out. You need to become a laser-sharp marksman focusing on a very specific micro-niche.

For thousands of years, people only did business with those who were geographically close to them. They bought from the baker down the road, the accountant nearby and went to their local toy store. In a world where geography was a natural barrier, a "general store" approach works well because you can capture as many people as possible in your local vicinity.

Today we live in a world unlimited by geography. We are connected to each other with the swipe of a finger on a smart phone. People now buy from the companies they find when searching on their iPad, regardless of where the business is geographically located.

For this reason, you need to focus. You need to become known for the micro-niche and be prepared to sell to people wherever they are. The "general store" is Amazon and you're not going to beat them at their game. Instead you'll use their technology to reach people all over the world.

Your micro-niche is something you pitch for. Whenever you are asked, "What do you do?" You share exactly the type of thing you are aiming for. No more boring, general answers; from now on, go directly after the perfect client or project you want to work with.

## Constructing a social pitch

The age old question, "What do you do?" can lead to a deep conversation or it can lead to polite, but disengaged chit-chat. Your goal is to prepare a short answer to this question that lights people up and has them asking for more.

### Here are ten general, boring answers to the question, "What do you do?"

1. "I'm a consultant. I help businesses grow."
2. "I have a PR agency. We work with brand endorsement deals."
3. "I have a financial services business that provides advice."
4. "I have a training company that deals with HR issues."
5. "I design websites, blogs and e-commerce platforms."
6. "I'm a personal fitness instructor and I help people to lose weight or tone up."
7. "I'm a chartered accountant, but don't hold that against me!"
8. "I make furniture and other goods."
9. "My wife and I are starting up a business doing travel related services."
10. "We shoot video for businesses. We can do anything relating to film production, editing, animation... stuff like that."

All ten of those answers will get a polite response from the person who asked you what you do. None of them will get you any real business. None of them will open up the floodgates of opportunity.

Those answers are boring and general. They don't really exclude anyone and they create no density or gravity that attracts people to what you do.

## Here's how they could improve the previous ten answers:

1. "I help companies grow by buying their competitors business. I built my own company through acquisitions and sold it for a large sum. A lot of the deals I do involve almost no cash and my clients often double their revenue in a single deal."

2. "I run a PR agency. We specialize in matching celebrities to products. The deals we create make tons of money for everyone involved, and last years. We don't just work with big companies; we also have celebrities who can help smaller businesses to grow in exchange for equity."

3. "I run a finical services firm. We have fifty highly qualified people on our team who do nothing but crunch data on investments and risk. We then sell advice to some of the world's biggest investment funds. Our mission is to solve the retirement crisis facing baby boomers."

4. "I have a training company that teaches managers how to fire someone properly. We are experts in how to have difficult conversations and to how to fire people so that they feel okay about it. We save our clients a fortune in legal claims and we unleash high performance within their teams."

5. "My design agency creates blogs for non- fiction authors. We make stunningly good-looking blogs that people keep

coming back to again and again. This typically results in more paid speaking engagements, consulting opportunities and book sales."

6.   "I'm a fitness instructor. I take people on ten-day fitness retreats to Thailand to learn Thai-Boxing on the beach. People then come back and maintain a daily fitness program that my team manages."

7.   "I'm a chartered accountant. I work exclusively for consultants and contractors who are one-man-bands. I make sure their shoebox full of receipts actually gets filed and that they pay as little tax as legally possible. If a consultant is earning over $70,000 I can usually save them at least $3000 and two hours a week."

8.   "I create rare, exclusive, one-of-a-kind boardroom tables and desks. Our tables and desks often go up in value and are collected by billionaires and celebrities. Recently we were appointed to supply our work to one of the world's most exclusive brands."

9.   "My wife and I used to work for a major airline rewards program. We now work with small to medium sized businesses to maximize points programs so business owners can fly around the world in business class for free."

10.  "We shoot orientation and training videos that are designed to be shown to new members of staff in their first week. We capture stories about the values of your business and the specific things they need to know in order to represent your organization correctly from minute one. This can transform the culture of your organization and get your team to show more initiative."

These ten examples are loosely based on real-life successful businesses. As a result of improving that basic first response to the question, "What do you do?" They have generated a lot of business and opportunities in the real world, and they are more engaging than most people you'll meet.

## Building a strong presentation pitch

Once people are hooked by what you do, they will want more. The goal is to make time to deliver a presentation pitch. Unlike a social pitch, that is short and punchy, a presentation pitch could range from a few minutes to a few hours, depending on the circumstances, and can really delve into the value you offer.

A presentation pitch can't be left to chance. When you have a captive audience you must be prepared to cover your bases. You also can't sound ill-prepared. You must know your pitch so well that it comes from your heart more than your memory. This means you need to write out a presentation pitch, learn it and practice it until you own it. You know you have it when you can talk passionately about your topic for three minutes, or three hours, without much preparation. Getting to this point requires you to start with some structure.

Let's take a look at some key things you need to know about your pitch.

### Your pitch centers around solving a problem

People don't buy anything unless it solves a problem. They might not describe it that way; they might say they have a need, a want or a desire. The deeper truth is they only buy things that meet an unmet need. There is no value in coming up with an idea that doesn't solve a problem in a better way than is currently available. There's no point pitching an idea unless you understand what the problem is that you're able to resolve.

There are two types of problems that are particularly valuable to solve:

- Something people or businesses are already doing/buying which you can provide better, cheaper, more conveniently or with more emotional benefit;

AND/OR

- An unsolved problem people or businesses have or will have soon (as a consequence of technological, economic, political or social change), which you can predict and solve.

## A pitch must be grounded in reality

For your pitch to have real power and value for others, they need to see that your idea is based on a genuine insight based in reality. This means they want to know how you arrived at the ideas in your pitch.

Ideas based on reality are almost always born from one of these three insights:

- **A Customer Insight.** One day you might have been shopping for something and you couldn't find what you were after. The service you received was terrible, you discovered something shocking or you just knew that it could be done in a much better way; so you set out on a mission to right all the wrongs you saw as a customer.

- **A Technology Insight.** You spotted a way that technology can be created in a way that solves a real problem or offers a brand new benefit to people. You see that there's some new opportunity to combine your niche with a new technology and make life easier. Usually you're well experienced in this technology and you've spotted a new application for it.

- **An Industry Insight.** You know your niche so well that you've been able to figure out how things should be done better, faster, cheaper, more consistently or with more fun. You've seen the future and you're going to be the first person there.

## Your pitch must be aligned to your story

When people hear you deliver your presentation pitch, it must tell them more than just why this is a good idea; it must tell them why it's a good idea for you. For any idea to hold your attention long enough and gain traction, it must be aligned with your strongly held beliefs or else you will get bored with it. A great presentation pitch leaves people with the feeling that you were *born to do this*

I believe entrepreneurs and business leaders are able to use their skills and resources to expansively solve meaningful problems in the world. If I get involved in any business that is aligned to that mission I know I will stay energized. Whenever I have tried to go after a good idea that didn't really line up with my beliefs, I tired of it quickly and it fizzled into an expensive learning experience.

# Quick Exercise

What strongly held belief do you have that makes you perfect for your business or idea?

I strongly believe ...

## Your pitch must articulate the payoff

Your presentation pitch must articulate the benefits you bring to the person listening. Too many people talk about what they do, what they are good at, what they are experienced in or what they are qualified for. All of that is irrelevant if you don't translate it into a payoff for the person who's listening.

Kevin Harrington worked with the famous radio DJ Wolfman Jack to launch a music collection of 151 songs that had all been number one hits. The executives said, "These songs are so good they sell themselves," and proceeded to run an infomercial with the DJ just playing music and a phone number at the bottom of the screen. They were hoping people would buy the album as a result of loving the product.

Sales were abysmal and the project was turning into a disaster when Kevin stepped in and taught Wolfman Jack how to pitch. Between the songs, he articulated the benefits of owning the full album in a well crafted pitch. He talked about the way it makes you feel, the way he had hand-selected the music and only included number one songs, the cost savings and the fun of hosting a party with these songs. Immediately sales went through the roof and the project was a success. Even if you know how valuable your product is, don't leave it to your potential buyers to figure it out. Clearly articulate all of the benefits and the ultimate payoff.

A dentist should talk about creating the perfect smile, removing people from pain or extending the life of clean, youthful teeth. Lawyers should talk about protecting a business from a well-funded competitor, preventing someone from winning a spurious claim or ensuring the co-founders of a startup are energized and focused on the business rather than bickering over their percentages.

Kevin recommends you have three core benefits that others will experience as a result of your business or your product.

For example, when I explain the Key Person of Influence method I extrapolate the three big payoffs:

1. You get to earn more money with less struggle.

2. You get more recognition within the industry you love.

3. You get to attract more of the right opportunities that energize you.

If people understand the payoff, they are interested in how to get it. Even if you have an amazing product, people won't buy from you if they can't figure out what it means to their life. It's best to link your product to the classic highly valued payoffs – more money, more time, better quality of life. Be as specific as you can.

## Quick Exercise

What three payoffs do you want to give to others?

## Your pitch can be delivered upon

Once we know *why* you want to do something and *what* it will do for people, the big question most people want to know next is *how* you will deliver it.

Will this be a consumable product? Will it be a service? Will it come as a subscription? Is it a training program? Is it a web site? Will it be a retail store? How you get your value to others may be in many forms and it may grow over time.

British billionaire entrepreneur Richard Branson has a big *why*: "To shake up old industries and give customers a more delightful experience." His Virgin empire delivers three main promises: 1) to give customers a better deal; 2) to make its service fun, and 3) to champion the needs of customers. How they deliver it is through trains, planes, credit cards, phones, festivals and about 150 other businesses.

## Quick Exercise

How do you deliver these three valuable payoffs?

## Constructing your presentation pitch

When you know the foundations of your pitch, life and business gets easier. With strong foundations in place, you can easily give a talk, write a brochure, create a new product, author a book, record a video or make a deal. The most important next step is using these foundations in a nice logical order to share your ideas with others in a way that allows them to buy into your vision.

There are many ways to structure a pitch. The first method I teach people when they are new to pitching is fairly basic.

### Position yourself as clear and credible:

It's clear to your audience who you are and why you are worth listening to. You might state something that reinforces this yourself, you might be introduced by a respected friend, you might arrive in your private jet (as any billionaire will tell you, the real value of a private jet isn't the leg room).

## Articulate the problem and how you noticed it:

You have seen a real problem and you are calling attention to it. Sara Blakely the billionaire founder of Spanx tells her story of being frustrated with normal panty-hoes in a hot Floridian climate. She liked the way they made her body look firmer, but didn't like the seams and the way they rode up. As a result she created an undergarment that is seamless, firming, has an open toe, but stays where it should.

## Extrapolate on the impact of the problem:

You know that this problem impacts more areas of life than one might first think. You project forward into the future and stipulate what implications can arise if this problem isn't dealt with.

## Solve it:

Suggest that you have a way of solving this problem and share your ideas freely. Educate people on the key insight you have for making sure this problem is solved properly.

## Prove it:

Back up your claim with some proof that it's a good idea; if you don't have proof you can have a highly respected person vouch for what you are saying. Quote some statistics if you can or share a case study that ads weight to your message.

## Ask for what you want:

Finally, share what you need from them in order to take the idea forward. Be specific, be bold and be clear about what you want and why.

**Leave people uplifted:**

Don't finish a pitch on a flat note. You want to finish with a story, an idea or a vision for the future that gets people excited. People don't often remember everything you said, but they surely remember the way you left them feeling. Be sure to deliberately leave people feeling positive.

Use this structure to write out a pitch and rehearse it. It might seem a little too structured at first; however, with practice you will develop so much clarity in your own mind that you will be able to talk about your idea naturally and still hit these bases in the right order.

If your pitch sounds too rehearsed, you haven't rehearsed it enough.

## Pitching Bonus: Public speaking and media appearances

One of the fastest and most powerful ways to become a Key Person of Influence quickly is to speak to groups, either at live events or through the media. As a speaker or media personality, you are instantly transformed into an authority on you topic and you reduce the time it takes to get your message out.

One of the essential things all Key People of Influence must do is to feel comfortable giving their pitch to a group. This will only happen if you've practiced your pitch one-on-one with hundreds of people. The more you give your pitch to the people around you, the more likely it is that you'll be given an opportunity to leverage your message. It's virtually impossible to make it into the media or onto the stage if you can't deliver a powerful pitch to an individual first.

If the thought of public speaking or being featured in the media scares you, consider enrolling on a speaking course or working with a professional to ensure you can get your message across to a group as powerfully as you can in a one-to-one meeting. No one is born with speaking skills. The insider secret is that every great pitcher, speaker or media personality has had training. Organize your pitch into a talk and ready yourself for the day you get invited to take the stage or appear in the media. It will also help you in Steps Three and Four of the KPI Formula when you go to create a product and an online presence.

## Embrace the critics

A big fear people have when pitching their idea is getting what they perceive to be a negative response. Kevin hasn't just sold a lot of products, he's raised hundreds of millions of dollars for his businesses as well. He regularly explains to entrepreneurs one of the best responses you can get when you tell someone your idea is, "That won't work!" Rather than getting offended, he sees this negative reaction as an excellent opportunity to find out what people think is currently blocking the way forward.

If someone says to you, "That won't work," don't be offended, get curious. Ask them why they think it won't work. Be patient, ask lots of questions and write down the answers. It's these valuable insights that will draw you to discover the most important elements of your pitch that you need to get across.

You might get the chance to pitch to the perfect person and they might start picking holes in your plan. Don't fight them. Don't try to shut them down. Instead, get curious.

If someone says that it won't work because, "You won't find good staff who can deliver the specialized service," then your next pitch will become even more powerful when you say, "A big reason this hasn't been done before is because it's almost impossible to find the staff needed to deliver the service. We have been able to overcome that issue, and here's how...".

A typical startup entrepreneur wants people to love their ideas and hates it when someone points out even minor flaws in their plan. A more experienced leader realizes that a critical eye is a valuable thing and any shortcomings must be addressed in order to improve the plan. Of course you want people to be blown away by your pitch, but you're also pitching to get feedback and some of your best insights will come from your critics. For anyone who relished the criticism they gave you, it will be that much sweeter when you succeed after addressing their concerns.

## A perfect pitch powers performance

Your pitch is your foundation. It's the most basic asset you have as an entrepreneur, leader or change maker and it's also one of your most powerful.

Even larger companies benefit when every person knows how to pitch. One of our clients taught his 50+ team how to pitch properly. Everyone from the receptionist to the directors had to know the three-minute pitch by heart. The results were stunning, the entire company saw greater alignment, more energy, more innovation and more sales that could all be tracked back to this pitching activity.

Your pitch also forms the basis of the next steps in the KPI Method. From a great pitch you will be able to publish powerful content, invent hot products, build a trusted profile and get others involved through partnerships. Yet, without a powerful pitch, you should be cautious completing the next steps in this book (by all means read them, but just be sure that getting the pitch right happens first). If

your pitch has flaws they will show up in everything else you produce. A poor pitch will yield a boring book, products that are impossible-to-sell, websites that don't keep people reading and fruitless partnerships.

You want to be sure that what you have to say is valuable, you are excited by it and that others can get excited too (or easily see it's not for them). You want to be sure you are happy about your micro-niche and the part you want to play in it. You want to have tested your pitch on people who are in the know and gauged that they are in favor of your ideas.

If you're happy with what you have created, then get ready for the next step in the KPI Method. You are about to see how to get an express pass to the inner circle of your industry by writing and publishing your ideas.

## BONUS

For a special audio download relating to this section visit:
*www.keypersonofinfluence.com/pitch*

# STEP TWO: PUBLISH

When you have a perfect pitch, several big questions tend to come up for people (whether they say them out loud or not). They are thinking:

"Why should I listen to you?"

"How do I find out more?"

"How do I pass on this information?"

A lot of people come up with big ideas every day; however, very few people can attract the right team and see a project through to completion. The people you pitch to will want to learn more about the ideas you have and about you, personally.

People need to know that you are:

- Able to come up with credible insights, and
- Trust your ability to get things done.

Quality published content says a lot about you. A published book says that you have put enough thought into this idea to have written an entire book on the topic.

Published content online allows people to read your ideas and get to know your story from anywhere in the world. It allows someone to easily pass on information to others without the risk of setting up a face-to-face meeting.

Interviews and articles that you've written say that you must either be an expert or have access to experts. We assume that in order to write a quality article, you must have some expertise in this field or you must have been able to interview people with an expertise.

Very few people create a significant volume of published content. If you have articles, blogs, reports, case studies and a book, you are likely to be perceived as a Key Person of Influence in your industry.

You'd be shocked at how many of the world's biggest businesses started with published content. The founders of Twitter were bloggers and authors who were sharing ideas about the future of social media long before their platform was even conceived. Bill Gates wrote articles for his local computer clubs and attracted the first talented employees to Microsoft because of what he wrote. Even established leaders and entrepreneurs take their game to the next level by writing and publishing.

Kevin found his way onto the show *Shark Tank* because of his first book, *Act Now!* After his book was published, Kevin was invited onto several radio shows to talk about his journey as an entrepreneur. Reality TV Producer Mark Burnet heard Kevin on radio and ordered the book. After reading the book, he contacted Kevin and invited him to be one of the millionaire investors on the show. From there, Kevin was able to earn millions from the 100+

deals he invested in; not to mention the added advantage of being a celebrity entrepreneur across the USA.

Facebook executive, Sheryl Sandberg wrote the book, *Lean In*, and is now considered to be the world's most sought after CEO. Richard Branson is dyslexic and manages to release a new book every other year. Donald Trump used his first book to step out of his father's shadow and establish his own personal brand.

## Commit to writing a book

For the rest of this section I want to encourage you to write a book on your topic. It requires you to produce about 30,000 – 50,000 words and cover a range of relevant information. You'll write case studies, stories, methods and all sorts of valuable insights in the process of producing a book.

A published author is often well connected in their field. In writing a book, you will be able to pick up the phone and talk to all sorts of new contacts to get input for your book. If you have published something, chances are that you are able to attract the right people around you.

Imagine when you meet people and say, "I am the author of a book on my industry, and while writing the book, I discovered a potential business opportunity that I am currently working on." Now people are interested. This wasn't just anybody who came up with an idea; it was the author of a book. And if this person has what it takes to write a book, they could clearly start a business in that field, too.

You might be a bit worried about writing an entire book. Maybe you believe you don't have enough content to fill a book. Maybe you think your ideas aren't special enough in your opinion. Maybe you feel your ideas aren't worth writing about. These are all concerns that many now-published authors had before sitting down and writing their books and articles.

A friend of mine is a writing coach. In addition to writing several books himself, he has helped hundreds of people to plan, write, publish and promote their books. He has absolutely convinced me that there is a book in everyone if they follow a process and commit to its completion. If it happens that you fall short of a book, you'll be able to repurpose your content into reports, articles, blogs, hand-outs and the like. So for now, set a goal to write a book.

## Why publish your book?

A book is a powerful document to create. In the process of writing all those words, you will clarify your thinking, exhaust your ideas and generate intellectual property. When you publish it, you'll be one of the few people who can find their own creation on Amazon.

The first thing you should do is construct some real reasons why you want to write a book. Is it because you want the money? Do you want the "bestselling author" title? Do you want to be featured in the media? Do you want to create something that will outlast you? Maybe you trust this process enough to write your book because we've told you to! These are all good reasons to write a book, and I am sure you will have some other reasons that will excite and motivate you.

It's important that you get clear on the benefits you want to achieve from your book before you begin the process. When the writing gets tough, you need to be able to imagine yourself getting the things you want out of life as a result of your published book.

## Different types of books

Fortunately, there are a few different types of books you could write and each one has unique benefits.

Here are five types of books you could write:

### 1. Thought leadership

This is a book you can write based on your story and your background; it's full of your ideas and insights. This book is "your take on things."

People on the KPI Program have produced books like:

*Honey Let's Buy A Boat - Everything you wanted to know about buying and owning a powerboat but didn't know to ask.*

*Six Pack Chicks - Change Your Mind, Transform Your Body.*

*Naked Divorce - The 21 Day Program For Your New Life.*

The advantage is that it gives you plenty of room to demonstrate your ideas and your unique take on things. You are the star of this kind of book, because it's you sharing your insights and perspective.

## 2. Book of interviews

This is a book where you find existing KPIs and feature their stories or their ideas in a book. I was featured in the book, *Secrets of My Success*, a compilation of stories from entrepreneurs who the author considered to have achieved remarkable results. The author of this book, Jamie X. Oliver, interviewed dozens of people to construct his book.

The advantage of this type of book is that it's a great reason for you to get to know existing KPIs in your industry. Very few people can resist the idea of being featured in a book and most will happily sit for hours answering your questions. You may even be able to record the interview and make it into a product (more on that later). The disadvantage is that you don't get to be the star of the show. Your KPI status will improve as a person who must be well connected, but not as a thought leader yourself.

## 3. Book of tips

This is a book full of quick tips and rapid fire ideas. A great example is a KPI Program client, JP DeVilliers who wrote, *ReShape: 77 Ways To Reshape Your Body and Your Life.* He's a fitness trainer who had limited time between clients in the gym. He allocated three short slots throughout his day to note down a tip and by the end of the month he had his book.

To write this sort of book, list off the ten main categories of interest you want to cover, then come up with ten tips for each category. Now you will have 100 tips. It will take you less than two months to write the book if you complete three tips per day.

The disadvantage is that these books, if not crafted correctly, can seem a bit scattered or may appear not to delve deep enough into a topic. The advantage is that type of book is fun and easy for your reader to dip into; it's also an easier format for you to write. It's also easy to repurpose each tip as a blog or magazine article.

## 4. Picture book

For some industries you might be better off showing pictures rather than words. Clearly if you are a photographer or a fashion designer, people would be much more interested in pictures.

A KPI Program client, John Cassidy, is one of the world's top headshot photographers. His book, *7 Mistakes People Make with Their Headshot Photos*, is a series of before and after photos that illustrate the difference between a great headshot and a poor one. Including his tips and his philosophies with the photos, this short picture book serves as a perfect business tool.

The advantage is that people love looking through picture books and they tend to sit on coffee tables rather than book shelves. It's also an easy book to create in short runs through a number of online picture book publishers. The disadvantage is that this book probably needs to be printed in high-quality color, using high-resolution photos, and it can get costly to produce.

## 5. A creative piece

This could be a parable with a message or a fictional story. The advantages are that you get full license to make up as much as you like and that it's very much an expression of your creativity. People love creative books; fiction massively outsells non-fiction.

A good example is the book, *If Your Body Could Talk: Letters from your body to you*, by KPI Program client, Jacqui Sharples. It's a series of letters written from a woman's body to the woman who "owns" it. The book is powerful and compelling; it's hard to put down and it has a profound impact on everyone who reads it. It works because Jacqui is a gifted writer and her message isn't lost in this format; if anything it's turned up even more.

The downside is that few people are skilled enough as a writer to get this genre right, and it has little value to you as a Key Person of Influence if the message doesn't come across. My opinion is to leave this genre to the pros unless you feel a strong calling to write this style of book.

## The message of the book

Once you have decided on the type of book you will produce, it is very important to consider the message you want your reader to walk away with. My writing coach says that a great book must answer at least one significant question that the reader is trying to answer.

Your readers may be asking themselves:

"How do I have difficult conversations with an employee?"

"How do people become wealthy, starting from scratch?"

"How do I protect my valuable business ideas?."

The reader's core question forms the theme of your book, and each chapter, interview or section gives another key piece of information that answers this question.

## Planning the book

Before you even lay your fingers on the keyboard to start writing your book, you must plan your book.

When you plan your book, you put the key question on a large piece of paper and brainstorm all of the connected questions people in your micro-niche might ask. Explore the content you need to share with them to fully answer their questions. When you've done that, you need to arrange your ideas into chapters and then brainstorm your chapters in the same way. If you spend one to two hours really mapping out each chapter, writing the book is a breeze.

The more you plan out your book, the easier it is to write creatively and the better your book will be. Some people prefer big sheets of paper and others like to plan their book using excel spreadsheets. Find a way that works for you and spend a considerable time on the planning stage.

Planning your book is also an excellent exercise for your mind. Mark Twain famously said, "The time to begin writing an article is when you have finished it to your satisfaction. By that time you begin to clearly and logically perceive what it is you really want to say." His sentiment is that the writing process makes you smarter. A big part of that process is to plan it out. The clearer your thinking around the book, the easier it is to be creative. Through careful planning you can formulate your vague thoughts into clear, articulate and tangible ideas that will spread.

## Choosing the title of your book

Whatever type of book you produce, one of the most important decisions is the title. Many more people will hear that you are the author of "The Title You Chose," than those who actually read the book.

You might like to call your book something vague that only makes perfect sense once read to the end. However, your book will lose impact with a cryptic title. If you introduce yourself by saying, "I am the author of the book *The Race*, people can't tell what you are a Key Person of Influence in. If you introduce yourself as "the author of *The Race Towards Green Energy*," people instantly understand that you must be a KPI for green issues.

Don't wait until you have the perfect title before you create your book. Quite often several titles will hit you while you're writing. Often ideas for other books will hit you. However, I would encourage you to make them chapter titles in your first book.

When you're ready, make a list of at least five potential titles and run them past a few people to see which elicits the best response. Go to a networking function and tell people you're writing a book called, "_____." Watch their response and see if they want to put you in touch with some relevant people. If so, you're onto a winner.

My belief is that you should choose a title that reinforces that you are a Key Person of Influence. It should be brand enhancing and you should feel proud to tell people that you are the author of that book.

Some of the great book titles created on the KPI Program by our clients are:

*Legally Branded* – Shireen Smith

*Winning Client Trust* – Chris Davies

*Process to Profit* – Marianne Page

All of these titles have been perfect for getting across the message that the author is a Key Person of Influence in their chosen field.

## Environment dictates performance

I recommend getting a writing coach or joining a writing group so you have access to feedback, accountability and guidance. The Key Person of Influence Program we run all over the world has a huge success rate for getting people to perfect their pitch and then turn it into a book in a matter of a few months. People who join the Key Person of Influence Program are provided with a coaching, mentoring and accountability through the book writing process and many are shocked to see a completed manuscript in under thirty days.

As with anything challenging, being part of the right environment is half the battle. You want to be part of an environment that normalizes the result you are seeking. If you want to be better at tennis, join a tennis club or get a tennis coach. If you want to make more money, hang out with people who earn lots of money. If you want to write a book, get around people who are also writing a book. The accountability of having someone coaching you and being part of a group who are all writing is a powerful formula for getting your book out.

There is a lot to learn about writing a book and getting it to sell. It's worth working with someone who's done it before. So many people say they are "working on a book," but few actually get it published.

Don't get caught in the trap of getting half way through several book ideas. The book has no power until it's finished. A writing program can help you to get your book completed and on Amazon in under six months rather than thirty-six months. Imagine what an extra thirty months of being a Key Person of Influence is worth.

## Publishing your book

In the past, getting a publishing deal was an essential part of becoming an author. Only publishing houses had the money and the power to print a large quantity of books and then get them distributed. Today there are boutique printers and small publishers who will print your book

in very small runs on demand. There's no reason you can't print just twenty copies of your book at a time.

In the past, it was also pointless writing a book without a publishing deal in place because you simply couldn't get it distributed. Today you can have your book distributed worldwide through Amazon, iTunes and other sites. You can set up an author account online in a matter of minutes, and within a week your book can be shipping all over the world from Amazon's warehouses. More importantly, when people google your name they can see that you are an author on page one of the results.

Although it might seem glamorous to be published by a big name publisher, many Key People of Influence today are choosing to self publish so that they can make more money from books when they sell or give them away more cheaply.

## Promoting your book

There are many ways to promote your book if you want to focus on marketing; however, it is not vital that your book is a massive seller. It is more important that you are an author. Each year less than a dozen books sell over a million copies. Most books don't sell more than 500 copies a year.

That's fine! If you use your book correctly, it won't need to sell millions. The mere fact that you are an author and that people can see you on Amazon gives you more kudos and opportunities.

You will find that it is easier to get invited to speak, to get publicity in the media and to get face-to-face with key contacts once you are an author. Being an author helps you to become known as a Key Person of Influence. When you meet people you can gift them a copy of your book. You can give your existing clients several copies to give to their friends. Both these ideas don't sell any books, but will still help you make more money.

In later chapters, I will share some social media strategies to promote your book. But it is completely acceptable if your book only sells a few dozen copies each year. Remember, it is not authors who get great opportunities, it is KPIs. Your goal is to become the Key Person of Influence in your industry in under twelve months, not to spend all your energy trying to sell books. Without all five steps in the KPI Method, you'll miss out on the bigger picture. The purpose of your book is to promote you, not the other way around.

## Publishing articles

As I mentioned, the reason I've focused on writing a book up until now is because once you have the content written you can repurpose it in many ways. Of course, you could also approach things the other way around and write articles and blogs first and later use these as chapters in your book.

An article, if published in the right place, can be incredibly powerful for building your brand and communicating with your market. Kevin writes for *Forbes Magazine* and is regularly featured on their website as an expert entrepreneur. Each article is seen by tens of thousands of people and generates all sorts of opportunities. It would be impossible to create a fresh book every month and promote it to a mass market, but it's easy to create a wide reaching message as a blogger or magazine contributor.

One of the KPI Program clients, who owned a flight school, published a set of articles about his "WWII Spitfire Project," and it brought enquiries in from around the world. He had a goal to build a squadron of replica Spitfires and the article was instrumental in finding other interested parties and making it happen. Writing these articles forced him to get very clear about his ideas and gave him an excuse to interview relevant KPIs in his industry. After his articles were published in a boutique flying magazine, he was able to send copies to his existing clients and gain the credibility that comes with being published in an industry magazine.

Rather than just typing up a single article, I would urge you to at least write a set of ten articles, each 1000 to 1500 words in length before you even begin to talk to publications. By writing a set of ten articles, you still get the benefits of fully exploring your unique ideas and you can get in touch with a wide range of key people for interviews. You also get the chance to pitch several options to a publication, and if they like your work, you are ready to follow up with more content. Be sure to collect any publications you are in, scan the front page along with your contribution and put it on your web site and on your social media profiles.

A book is a very valuable way to publish your ideas; however, if it's genuinely not right for you at this time, get started on creating your set of articles ready for publication.

## Publishing creates credibility — Products create cash

Your book, articles, blogs or reports will be brilliant tools for getting your thinking clear, for getting recognized as credible, and for connecting to the right people. However, there's not much money in it directly. Well designed products are the key to making money, so rather than pushing yourself to sell more books or to get paid as a writer, let's move along and explore how to create hot products that bring in the money.

## Are you ready for the next step?

In the next chapter you will see that a great product can be high-value, low-cost and open up all sorts of opportunities. If you are ready to turn your skill set into an asset, read on.

## ACTION STEP

For some additional content on this step visit:
*www.keypersonofinfluence.com/publish*

# HALFWAY POINT

How are you going with the hidden theme?

You are halfway through this book; have you found it yet?

Keep looking, keep connecting the dots and if needed, re-read this book a few times until you get it. The theme I'm talking about is something you are very close to, maybe it's something you've taken for granted until now. Consider this theme I'm talking about might have something to do with your story and this book may only be a tool for finding it. Maybe the theme I'm referring to started long before you even picked up this book. Look back in the early chapters, see what you can remember.

Life has a funny way of trying to get something done no matter what you do.

# STEP THREE: PRODUCT

## Money moves towards hot products

Why does Apple have lots of money? For over ten years they have produced very hot products. If they fail to do that in the future, the money will dry up for them.

Why do oil and gas companies have lots of money? For over 100 years oil and gas has been a very hot product. If we create more solar energy technology, the oil and gas companies will lose their hot product and they will lose their money.

Why did Kevin Harrington make a fortune? Because he knew how to create hot products. He figured out how to turn something from a good idea into a must-have device that you'd buy on impulse.

What about you? The reason you've made money in the past is because of products, too. Maybe you started by selling your time to an employer. Maybe you then started selling services to your clients. Maybe you've made money buying and selling a house. Any of these money makers were actually about products. Your time was a product that an employer wanted, your services produced something your clients wanted and your house went up in value as it was seen to be a hotter product than before.

Maybe in the future you'll have other products to sell that you've not yet created. Maybe your business will sell products that are so hot you'll make more money than you can spend in your lifetime. Your business will really take off when you have several products that spread your message and expand your income opportunities.

## Product ecosystems

Here's a powerful idea to consider – *Products and services don't make money, product and service ecosystems do.* Your business will really take off when you have a mix of products and services that all work together to maximize the value exchange in every customer relationship.

Businesses that make lots of money can't put their finger on which product makes them the money. They give away some digital products for free, some things they sell cheaply, some products or services are high value but they only sell to warm prospects who received the free product. Kevin became well known as the inventor of infomercials, but his empire boomed when he had a steady flow of products moving from TV into retail stores and then online.

Imagine if Google started charging for search, maps or browsers. They'd probably lose their market share. It makes sense for them to give some things away and charge for others.

Some products are designed to build a relationship. Some products are designed to educate. Some products are designed to implement an idea. All hot products are based upon your insights.

## Products are packaged up ideas

We now live in a global economy that is largely intangible and centers around ideas more than things. The successful people who make money and win the accolades are the people who have powerful ideas and can turn them into products. The most valuable commodity on the planet today is called Intellectual Property (IP). The biggest companies on the planet are valued almost entirely on their IP.

A product is merely a valuable insight or an idea that has been packaged up so that people can access it easily, repeatedly and in a desirable way. We live in a time whereby products are the new marketing and advertising tools. In the past, companies would make fairly generic products and then spend a fortune telling the world that they were the best. Today that doesn't work. People have learned to tune out loud advertising and go looking for great products instead.

One of my favorite authors, Seth Godin, says,

> *"Finding new ways, more clever ways to interrupt people doesn't work. It's the person who knows how to create an idea that spreads that wins today."*

Kevin built his empire on infomercials; today, he invests into products that grow virally through word-of-mouth.

Rather than over-spending on ads, the better way is to create unique products that people want to access and talk to their friends about. If you create a valuable product, your customers and clients will tweet, share, blog, update and "like" it publicly and do your marketing for you.

## Digital products

One of the best ways you can really share your ideas with a vast number of people in an effective way is to create a digital product. This will likely be a download or an online tool. Such products are not an interruption; they are a means of communication that consumers chose to participate in. If packaged correctly, such products have a high perceived value even though the cost to reproduce them is almost nothing.

If someone takes an hour to listen to your audio podcast, they feel rapport with you, they bond with you and really start to understand what makes you unique. If someone takes your online training program, they've already begun to buy into your ideas. If someone joins your membership, books onto your webinar or takes your online test they are spending money and getting to know you. You start becoming the person they *must* do business with rather than a person they *could* do business with. You shift from functional to vital.

## Productized services

A service can be packaged up like a product. You can give your service a name, it can have a method, it can have a brochure, it can be delivered by other trained professionals. This productized service could include elements that are standardized and elements that are custom made. Don't fall into the trap of thinking you deliver a service and this step can't apply to you. Treat your service like a product and you'll see an uplift.

A plastic surgeon who joined the KPI Program thought he would struggle with product creation because it doesn't get more individualized than performing surgery. However, he was able to give his method a name, create brochures, compile testimonials and add additional complimentary products into the overall bundle. As a result, his value went up and his waiting list grew.

You're service is part of the product ecosystem, so be sure to make it as productized as you can and to surround it with other products that help educate, inspire or relate to more people.

## Physical products

Don't underestimate the value of a uniquely valuable physical product for your business. Kevin Harrington discovered the "Great Wok of China" from his friend Wally Nash who'd been to Asia on a product tour. The Wok was similar looking to most pots and pans at first glance, but it had a unique feature. Each wok was hand hammered 6000 times to create tiny little ridges and those ridges evenly distributed the spices and sauces through the food. The wok was sold with a recipe book and utensils for forty dollars per unit and Kevin's company sold forty-five million of them. Communicating a simple but unique idea through a physical product made Kevin ten million dollars in profit!

There's never been a better time in history to invent or source physical products. Not too long ago, if you wanted to create a physical product, you had to get on a plane to China, hire an interpreter, a guide and do tours of various factories. For many people this ended in disaster. They overpaid, the quality wasn't what they expected or they simply wasted time and money without finding what they were after. Today with websites like *alibaba.com* you can tour all the factories to get exactly what you want and to customize it any way you can imagine.

Be aware though, it's not a physical product on its own that is valuable; it's the ideas and insights that are communicated through that product that will set it apart.

## Products expand your income opportunities

Imagine that you get invited to be a guest speaker at a seminar for thirty minutes (random invitations to speak are quite common for an author). You agree, on the condition that you can promote your digital product for fifty dollars. At the end of the talk, you say, "If you like what you just heard and you want to know a little more, I have a special offer for my online training program."

If twenty people out of the group decide to buy, you just got paid $1000 for a thirty-minute speaking spot; a great result. This may also lead to a lot more business. Each person who buys the first product is more likely to want to do business with you in the future as well. Rather than it being logged as an expense to talk at a local function, your product allows you to become a highly paid speaker and continue the relationship with all the people who enjoyed your talk.

## Products don't sleep

If *you* are your only product, being paid for your time, this presents a big problem. You only want to work for about a third of the day and you can only be in one place at any given time. There will always be a limitation on what you can earn if your earning capacity is based solely on your personal appearance.

Products are expansive and liberating because you can sell them online twenty-four hours a day, seven days a week, and they can be delivered all over the world. This one fact alone is a key reason you must develop a product on your journey as a Key Person of Influence.

Selling your time may still be part of what you do, but when you have products, the value of your time goes up not down. Additionally, you only do the high value work that you probably enjoy.

## Every business has ideas behind it

You may be wondering how "product thinking" applies to a more traditional business like commercial cleaning, photocopying, stationary or logistics. Should these more unglamorous businesses create an information product for their clients too? Absolutely, *yes*.

Regardless of the business, it is the ideas behind your business that make it special and prevent you from having to constantly compete on price. In order for any business to stand out from the crowd, it needs to have some great underpinning ideas. People want to know what sets you apart or, at the very least, your perspective on things before they get excited about you and feel happy to spend a little more.

Imagine a dry cleaner that gave you an app that told you what to do immediately if you stained your cloths. You'd keep that app on your phone and you'd think about your dry cleaner as soon as you spilt something on your shirt.

Imagine a men's fashion outlet that had an online video series featuring an image consultant sharing ideas on, "How To Look Slimmer, Richer and More Powerful For Less Than $500." Instantly, you start thinking about spending $500 with that store.

Imagine a restaurant that had recipe book from the chef with chapters that reveal her commitment to sustainable, ethical farming. You'd talk to your foodie friends about it. Just seeing a chapter called, "Why I choose to pay more for my ingredients so that you can feel good about your meal," would make you feel good about paying a little more at the end of your night.

No matter what industry you are in, you need to share the ideas that make you special. Explain to people what's so special about the way you deliver your service. Give them a peek behind the curtain at some of the things you take for granted, but your customers never knew.

The clients I've worked with have produced things they never knew they could and it transformed their business. They've created events, trainings, books, CDs, online tests, podcasts, apps and many other products that are designed to spread the word while making money.

## Creating your product

There are several types of products that can be useful for your business. The real uplift in income comes from several products and services that all work together. A "product ecosystem" creates a lot more money than any one product or service on its own.

There are two types of products you'll need to develop:

- Products that spread ideas and allow you to get known by more people.
- Products that deliver high value and make significant profits.

Let's take a look at these two types of products.

## Start with products that spread ideas

Everyone should have a free product. The person who will dominate your industry in the next ten years will be the one who is able to give more away for free than anyone else. The fastest growing companies in the 2000s were all companies that gave away incredible value for free—Google, Facebook, Twitter, LinkedIn. The best thing you can give away for free is an information product that educates people as to why they should do business with you.

## A free audio podcast

It's remarkably easy to record and upload an audio podcast. As soon as you do, you'll have a free product that's available all over the world. When people listen to it they are thinking, "This person really knows their stuff," or "This person is super connected," and they will want to do business with you.

There's nothing you can create more cheaply that has more value than an information product that shares your experience and insights with your potential clients. A podcast is free, it's valuable, it's global and it's fast. There's already a global audience downloading podcasts just waiting for yours to arrive.

## An information kit

An information kit can be something you sell online or offline. I know a couple who built a successful eBay business turning over about $400,000. They then created an information kit on how they set up their eBay business, sourced products and marketed them. That information kit generates over 1.2 million!

An information kit usually has workbooks and training resources. It could be something that is a standalone product or something that accompanies a live training.

Consider what you know that you could turn into an instructional guide. Is there something people already ask you to teach them? If it comes up again and again, it could be an indication to you that there are people all over the world who want to know these answers too.

## A webinar series

Webinars are online seminars or panel discussions that people can tune into from anywhere in the world. They are free or very cheap to set up and they have an impact.

Sometimes you don't even need to be brilliant in order to create a brilliant webinar. If you are able to secure an interview with some of the top people in your industry, you'll have hundreds of people interested in being on your webinar. Be sure to record it and produce set of interviews as part of your podcast. You'll become a KPI by association if you interview enough of the top experts in your industry.

## Here's a secret: share your secrets

Here's a big secret. Don't keep secrets. Share your best ideas with everyone.

Consider that the most famous chefs share their recipes every week. The more they share, the more their value goes through the roof. You don't hear people saying, "Now I have Jamie Oliver's recipe, I will never visit any of his restaurants again."

The more people have, the more they want, so share your ideas freely. You will also make room in your mind to have even better ideas. If you share powerful ideas, people will come to you to implement them and you can have a valuable service offering that does that.

## Niche products are higher value

If you want to sell an information kit on some general subject like, "How to be a good parent," it probably won't move. However, if you have honed your micro-niche and created a product like, "How to be an amazing single parent, while still working your high-pressure, city job," you will find that parents with this same challenge will beat down your door.

People spend a lot of time and money producing lame-duck products that lack value because they are too general. If you create a product that helps solve a very real and specific challenge that people have, it will perform. An example is "City-Kitty" a training program for teaching cats to use a regular toilet rather than a litter tray. This product seems strange, but it's a powerful idea that ended up getting free publicity on the major networks and cat owners raved about. It made Kevin over one million dollars in profit in under twelve months!

## High value products

After you've experimented with free or low cost products that get you known and spread ideas, you'll naturally want to create high value products that make serious money for you.

## Implementation, not ideas

Information is so readily available that its value has fallen considerably. Up until the 2000s, people would buy information and place a high price on it. They would pay hundreds of dollars for CD sets, seminars, videos, documents, reports and the like. Today all of that is freely available on any smart phone, so it's not something people will pay a lot for, if anything.

The real money comes from offering an implementation solution. At the same time information has fallen in value, the price of getting something done for you has risen. People are time poor and drowning in options. They want trusted suppliers who can get things done for them. This is where your "productized service" comes in to implement the ideas you've given away freely in your other products.

A top chef can give away recipes and strangely it drives demand for their restaurant. People read the recipe and then want the food made for them. It's the same in most industries. People listen to a fitness podcast then want to work with that trainer's company.

One of our KPI Program clients is a respected intellectual property lawyer. We helped her to create several informational products and to write a book. As a result, hundreds of people want her firm to advise on their business. She's created a productized service to streamline the process and to make her services available to people all over the world.

Another client of ours is a chiropractor. He used to sell his time by the hour and each time he would have to work hard to rebook the client. Working with us, he created a package product that included his services and the services of several other wellness professionals. This product gets better results for clients and all four practitioners are now easily selling each other's services every time they sell this product.

The key for these high-value products is that they are focused on implementation rather than ideas. Kevin and I personally give away a lot of ideas in books, blogs, articles, webinars and events. When time comes for people to implement these ideas, they will want to work with our team of professionals.

## Make a product for your competitors

There's also a lot of intellectual property that you take for granted that your "competitors" or counterparts (people like you who operate in different markets) would be interested in. Maybe your restaurant business is great at saving money on wasted food because you have a clever system you came up with. That product could earn you more profit than your restaurant does!

An industry-specific product can be worth a lot of money and make you one of the most respected people in your field, opening you up to joint ventures and partnerships. One of my clients figured out how to sell to millionaires who spend a lot more than typical clients. He now makes more money training his competitors how to win these clients than he does from his own high paying clients.

Keep in mind, even if you're selling a product to your competitors, it's the implementation they will pay more for rather than just the information.

## Ten intangible qualities of a successful product

New products flood the market daily. You can't help but turn on late-night TV and be confronted by one infomercial after another as you click through the channels. America's entrepreneurs are rolling out new ideas and new items faster than ever.

Millions of dollars are spent yearly developing and launching new products, but did you know that only one in ten will prove successful? And even fewer will enjoy a long shelf life. That's the cold reality, but you can greatly enhance your chances for business success if your product shares a series of ten intangible qualities separate from the physical product itself.

Kevin has helped launch more than 500 products, but he has suffered a few clunkers along the way. Here is the proven checklist of intangible features that he developed during his thirty years as an entrepreneur and investor.

The sizzle won't last if it doesn't stand up to this test. Ask yourself these ten questions before going public with your product or service:

1. "Is the product unique in its marketplace?" You can't roll out the "same-old, same-old." Your product has to have a cool new look that will make the consumer sit up and take notice.

2. "Does it have enough of a market who want it?" It's advantageous to target a micro-niche but there still has to be enough people who can afford to buy the product. Conduct some surveys to see if people want what you have and if there's enough to make it viable.

3. "Does it really solve a problem?" If your product doesn't solve a problem, you've got a potential problem – consumers aren't as likely to buy it. We all like to imagine people buying something just because they like it, but in reality people are more likely to buy things that solve problems.

4. "Is there a powerful offer with a competitive price?" The time-tested pitch– "But wait, there's more!" – is a proven winner. The key is great value at the right price. In today's world, people immediately check the Internet for the same product at a cheaper price.

5. "Can you easily explain how it works?" There has to be an easy-to-understand explanation of how and why your product works. Get your elevator pitch ready. If it takes a college degree to understand the pitch, it's too complicated. You may only grab people for a couple of seconds – so you

have to tease, please and seize their imagination.

6.  "Is there a magical transformation or demo?" Before-and-after images or statistics– showing easily noticeable differences – are powerful marketing tools.

7.  "Is it multifunctional?" Think like your competitor. If you come out with a product that has just one function, your competitor can steal your thunder – and your sales – with a similar product that offers more functions. Beat them to it and include the added function.

8.  "Are there credible testimonials?" An actual customer promo is ten times better than any actor portrayal. Real people offer real results. But you should also seek out professional testimonials from industry associations, doctors and other experts in your industry to further build your product's credibility.

9.  "Are there independently proven results?" Be prepared to back up your claims with unshakeable success stories or scientific studies, including third-party clinical studies or reviews from product-testing labs that support your claims.

10. "Can you answer the questions the buyer is thinking?" You must be prepared for any and all questions that could arise over your product. Put yourself in the shoes of consumers, and think of all the skeptical questions they could ask.

If you answered *yes* to all ten of these questions, you've got yourself a product that's solid and there's a good chance it won't land on the trash heap like the nine in ten that fail to catch on with consumers.

## You have a product – *Now what?*

Let's say for a minute that you've invented a widget – an app, a download, a physical product or a packaged service offering. You've spent hundreds of hours researching it, testing it, refining it, and now you're pretty sure that it's better than any other widget in the world.

Sounds like you've got it made, right?

Wrong! You're only halfway there.

A quick look through the history of entrepreneurship shows thousands of people who built great widgets and still managed to fail in spectacular fashion. Rudolf Diesel, Nicola Tesla, and Charles Goodyear all managed to die penniless, even as their inventions changed the world.

So how do you avoid becoming the Nicola Tesla of widget making? The solution is marketing, but not the old way.

Marketing is the crucial step between a great idea and a thriving business. It's how you convince people that your widget will make their lives better and is worth the price you're charging for it. Without an elegant way to take your products to market, they simply sit around the warehouse. You have no income, and without income, you quickly have no business.

Marketing in the twentieth century was fairly simple. Make your message appealing to as many people as possible, and then put that message in front of as many people as possible. It favored the big, the established, and the lowest common denominator. Many companies were built on that marketing model, but many who haven't changed with the times are suffering now.

We don't live in the twentieth century anymore. Communities are not dominated by the opinions of mass media gatekeepers like they were twenty or even ten years ago. The monolithic over-culture that used to turn on their televisions to watch *The Wizard of Oz*, the moon landings, and Nixon's resignation has splintered into countless thousands of individual tribes and communities. The gatekeepers of old have been cast down and now the marketplace is crowded with thousands of voices clamoring to be heard.

This isn't good and it isn't bad. It just means that you have to adjust your approach accordingly. It means that you have to be focused like a laser on *who exactly it is that will buy your product*. Anything else is a waste of time.

Is your widget designed for *professional* widgetteers? Then don't waste your time watering down your message to try and appeal to the hobbyist market. It's not going to work—there are already a hundred widgets designed specifically for hobbyists and yours will be too expensive and full-featured. The same goes the other direction; don't try and sell a hobbyist widget to professionals. They won't like its simplistic approach.

If your widget is waterproof, sell it to boat owners and scuba divers. If it's dishwasher-safe and childproof, sell it to parents. If it cuts payroll by ten percent, sell it to other business owners.

Today's market is all about the marriage of a unique product with the market of people who find it irresistible. Discover what makes your widget unique and who loves it for those reasons. Figure that marriage out and you really will have it made.

## Multiply your business valuation

A business is valued using a formula – *Value = Profit x Multiple*. For a business that owns its own unique products, that multiple is much higher than for a business that simply sells a service or brokers other people's products. Kevin has served on the board of five publicly traded companies and knows that the investor community places a lot of importance on the quality products a company is taking to market. If ever you have a desire to sell your business or raise investment, you'll get a better valuation thanks to the work you've done in creating hot products.

## Built to scale

We live in a digital age where it's actually cheaper to think globally than locally. The technology is now available for you to transfer your ideas, your pitch and your products to people anywhere in the world for free. I believe every business should be building products that could be delivered to people in cities around the planet.

Explore different ways to do this. It could be that you deliver your service over the internet, maybe you have local partners in several countries, perhaps you license your products into far away cities or maybe you travel the world and live the life of a high paid gypsy.

Whichever you decide, keep in mind that you'll start to attract interest from people all over the planet as you build your profile so you might as well be in a position to benefit from it. Likewise, if you don't know how to create a powerful presence online, then you will miss out on sharing your products with people who want them in parts of the world you never knew existed.

In the next chapter we make you "web-famous" so that when someone Googles you, they can see straight away you are a Key Person of Influence and they can begin to get excited to connect.

If you are ready to open up to opportunities all over the planet, turn to the next chapter and read on (after you complete the exercises, of course).

## ACTION STEPS

For bonus content relating to this step visit:
*www.keypersonofinfluence.com/product*

# Exercises

- What will your first podcast (or next one) be about?
- If you had a training workshop that people would pay $500 for, what would it teach people?
- What are the valuable insights that you could share on a downloadable report?
- What product could you sell to your competitors?

## Notes ...

# STEP FOUR: PROFILE

Key People of Influence are known, liked and trusted in their industry. It doesn't happen by accident; it takes a strategy and focused work to build your profile. You don't need to build a profile that makes you a household name in order to be seen as a Key Person of Influence, but you do need to become "web famous" when someone goes looking for you online.

Long before Kevin was on *Shark Tank*, he was "industry famous." In an industry that's known for speed, hustle and sometimes cut-throat behavior, Kevin was always careful with his reputation. As a result, he was usually the first person people would call when a hot deal came along. When people Google you, they want to see you are known, liked and trusted. They want to see videos, blogs, photos and groups you are part of. They want to be able to make friends with you, read your content and see the mutual friends and ideas you share. Nothing is more disappointing than meeting someone who seems interesting, but doesn't come up in a Google search. It makes people question your value. Over the past few years, we've come to believe that you are who Google says you are.

Everything we've covered until this point will already be helping to build your profile. A clear pitch is essential for building a profile, a book and articles raise your profile, and products create income opportunities that make building a profile viable. This step is about tying it all together so that when you are Googled by a respected KPI in your industry, they can see you're exactly the type of person they want to be working with.

## You have a rich media mogul uncle

Imagine that one day you get a letter from your rich uncle who just happens to be a billionaire media mogul. He's devastated that you have been estranged for all these years and he wants to make it up to you.

He says that all you need to do is video record yourself and he will distribute it worldwide for you for free on his network.

He says that if you record some audio, he will have it available on air all over the world.

He says that if you write an article, he will publish it and make it available in all corners of the globe.

What would you do? Would you write back and say,

"Sorry, I'm really a bit busy right now. I'm not good with technology and I've never done it before. I'd rather not promote myself to a global audience,. but thanks all the same."

If you are reading this kind of book, I'm sure you would drop everything to take up this great opportunity.

Well, the reality is that someone *is* making these offers to you. There are free opportunities to get your videos, audio, articles, images, and ideas out to the world right now through social media. Even better still, social media shares your ideas with people who are genuinely interested in them rather than trying to force them onto the mass market that doesn't really care.

A client of mine is known as, "The Posture Doctor." She's a chiropractic doctor who specializes in helping people correct poor posture. She launched a YouTube channel with posture correction advice and was shocked at the massive uptake; in the first year over one million people watched her videos. She focused her effort into a niche, she built a profile online and the opportunities came marching in.

## Why water the concrete?

Imagine setting up a watering system so that only ten percent of the water was landing on the grass. It would seem like a strange thing to do and yet many businesses will happily run advertising that targets a mere ten percent of readers. Why spend marketing money on ads that aren't right for ninety percent of the audience?

A typical $10,000 display ad in the newspaper is relevant to a small number of the readers so $9000 is just wasted. On top of that, your money has to pay for paper, journalists, delivery boys, news agents, managers, editors, ink, print presses and truck drivers. The cost of producing a real paper and getting it to people is huge.

Social media allows you to talk directly to your market and everyone else can go look elsewhere. It's also digital, so there are much lower costs of production and distribution. In short, social media allows you to have a long conversation with people who care about what you have to say for almost no cost whatsoever. You would be crazy not to use these powerful tools to promote yourself as a Key Person of Influence.

Allocate your marketing spend towards building a profile online with people who are actually interested. Rather than building a superficial profile with people who don't care, develop a deeper connection with the people who took the time to find you. It will bring about powerful results.

## Six objectives for building your profile

There are six clear business outcomes when building a profile both online and offline:

### 1. To generate leads and enquiries

Earlier I talked about the need to give away as much as possible for free. Social media allows you to give enormous value to the world for free and it comes back to you in the form of leads. Additionally, a lot of referrals these days happen through social media. Sites such as Wordpress, Twitter, Facebook and Slideshare are absolute gold mines for generating leads.

How many times have you heard someone say, "Google Fred Smith Limousine Hire" or "Look in my Facebook

friends for Mary Brown." You want to make sure that you get found when someone is recommending you! Traditional media also gets people calling, messaging, emailing and tweeting.

### 2. To convert leads and enquiries into sales

Imagine you go to a web site for an accountant. When you get there, you find videos to watch, audio downloads, photos, slides and blogs to read. Imagine you see a list of publications the business has been featured in and links to the stories. Is that going to make you more likely to do business with them? It sure is. Without a doubt, the more time a potential client spends with you, the more likely they will buy.

### 3. To increase the amount people spend

When people know more, they buy more. After years in sales and business, I have discovered that a buyer will spend about seven hours deliberating over a substantial purchase. Whether it is a big TV, a training course, a car, a three-month coaching program or an overseas vacation, consumers take about seven hours when you add it all up. If that's the case, you want to occupy as much of that seven hours as possible. You want them to be listening to your podcasts, watching your videos, following your Twitter feed and reading your blog posts.

As they do this, they're getting better educated on how much money they should be allocating to their purchase. Normally people start out thinking about getting the cheapest option, but with the right education they see the value in spending money on a higher quality product.

## 4. To increase the frequency of purchasing

In this busy world, people can simply forget about you. But not if they read your blogs, see your Facebook updates, follow your Twitter feed and subscribe to your YouTube channel. Keeping people up-to-date results in more purchases per client per year. If you email people every week they will unsubscribe and feel pestered by you. If they subscribe to your social media profiles, they look forward to your updates.

## 5. To find ways to reduce costs

Sure enough, you can use social media to reduce your printing and customer care costs, but the biggest savings is on what you would have spent on un-targeted advertising. Without social media, you might end up advertising in a local paper with less than ten percent of readers even remotely interested in what you offer; you end up paying for a lot of "eyeballs" that just don't care.

The beauty of social media is that it's free, or very low-cost, and it's targeted precisely at people who are interested in what you have to say.

### 6. To improve your overall brand

Having a great brand isn't only for big companies, your small business can also benefit. A consistent message that is all over the internet is a valuable thing when it comes time to raise investment funds or sell your business. It's also great for your team suppliers and joint venture partners to see. If ever you are criticized publicly, it helps to have built up a strong reputation to put any critique into a broader context.

## Becoming "Google-able"

When you Google search a KPI, it's clear who they are, what they look like (photos and videos), what they have to say and how to get in touch with them. It's not difficult to pass the Google test if you embrace social media because Google rates information on these main web sites highly. Some of the must-use sites you can use to make yourself web famous are (bear in mind that this list will probably date quickly):

- **YouTube.com:** The largest video broadcasting website on the internet. No one has to green-light your show, you upload it and you're ready for the world.

- **Slideshare.net:** The number one place to share your Microsoft PowerPoint and Apple Keynote slide presentations. You probably have some presentations already on your hard drive doing nothing; get them uploaded here.

- **Facebook.com:** The largest online social network, where you can have your profile and your business page. It's not just for silly photos and motivational quotes. A ton of business happens here.

- **LinkedIn.com:** The biggest online directory of professionals. Every day you can let your profile go out networking for you.

- **Wordpress.com:** An excellent place to host your blog, share ideas and use countless tools for building a profile and running a business online.

- **Twitter:** The micro-blogging site that is also an excellent place to listen to your customers and the industry leaders you admire.

Google will love you if you have a presence on these web sites and you take some time each month to keep your profiles up to date. You'll begin to see people coming your way when they search for your name or keywords in your profiles. Your followers, friends and fans will love you too, because they quickly get to know you through your videos, photos, groups and articles.

It's important to remember however, that your success online can only be as good as your pitch. If your message isn't strong, you'll

be wasting your time, or worse, you might even be damaging your brand. When it comes to content that you are putting online, be sure that it represents you well because you never know who's looking. Social media is like a microphone that amplifies you out to every corner of the world. Most people are too busy playing with the technology and go too far off message.

## The best is yet to come

Whatever you do, don't worry that you may have missed the boat on this new technology. It's just getting started. The first five years of social media was simply platform building and people were just using it for the fun of it. We will not see the full effects unfold for many years into the future.

I remember an elderly woman telling me about the excitement she felt when a new railway line connected her town to a big city as teenager. It wasn't the train or the tracks that was so exciting. The new railway line meant she was able to access a whole new world of possibility faster than ever before: new people, new ideas, new resources and new inspiration.

She wasn't the only one who saw the possibilities. After railway lines, highways, phones and air travel connected people in the first fifty years of the 1900s, a global boom in creativity occurred. By giving designers, engineers, entrepreneurs, investors and entertainers access to new markets, the world saw new music, entertainment, medicine, technology and products unfold to an unprecedented degree.

It is the same story throughout history. Before every boom in creativity comes a new way to connect: coaches, cars, phones, trains, planes. When humans can connect fast, we can create fast. Today, the world is buzzing with excitement as we see Facebook, Twitter, YouTube and Skype turn the big wide world into a standard feature in the living room.

However, let's not forget that the last ten years have seen technology focused on new ways to connect and share information at greater speed. This is the "railway line;" the real excitement comes from the fact that there is a whole new world of possibility on its way.

We are about to see the perfect environment for another boom in creativity. Designers, entertainers, entrepreneurs and everyone else can collaborate at a whole new level, faster than ever. An inventor in India can talk to an investor in London, who can pay for manufacturers in China to deliver a product in Sydney. All of this can be done easily and quickly, without big businesses slowing down the process.

There is no shortage of people talking about how bad things might be in the future; however, keep in mind that there is no shortage of new ways to make exciting progress either. Kevin and I predict a creative boom in art, entertainment, medicine, architecture, fashion and technology that we can barely comprehend right now. In every one of these fields there will be hundreds of micro-niches and in each little niche, there will be Key People of Influence.

Building your profile online and offline will tap you into these trends as they unfold. A great wave of innovation is happening. If you become known, liked and trusted you'll be surfing the wave rather than being swept out to sea.

After building a profile, the real trick is for Key People of Influence to connect in meaningful ways. KPIs need to connect with the right people and do deals that raise the value of everyone involved.

The next step is about partnership and it's often called the "money step." When you are ready to see how to make all your work pay off, turn the page for the final step in the KPI Method.

-----

## BONUS

There are some bonus materials on profile building here: *www.keypersonofinfluence.com/profile*

# STEP FIVE: PARTNERSHIP

What I am about to share with you is the secret that separates the KPIs who make real money and the people who look good, but still don't make the sort of money they are worth. The key is Partnerships. This is where you get to multiply time and rapidly achieve extraordinary results by working with other Key People of Influence.

Consider that someone has already built a relationship with thousands of people who could be your clients. That list is on someone's hard drive right now. Someone already has some free products that they would happily add to your product range just for the exposure. Those products are ready to ship right now. Someone already has a great brand and is looking for some great products to endorse. They are already more famous than you ever plan to be.

Just as you have worked hard in the last five years to create your pieces of the puzzle, someone else has worked just as hard and is holding onto the missing piece that you need. When the two of you connect up, the money can flow at an alarming rate. Kevin Harrington's success rests on partnerships. With celebrity endorsers, with inventors, with retail chains, with TV networks; it's all based on partnerships.

One remarkable partnership move Kevin made was to join forces with Guthy Renker Corporation and form a new company as a Joint Venture. Kevin's company Quantum and Guthy Renker, both had a ton of product deals that weren't right for either brand. By combining their strengths they spun out a new company, QGR, and it quickly made tens of millions of dollars profit that otherwise would have gone to waste.

In 2006, I first arrived in London with just a suitcase and a credit card, I literally knew no one. As an Australian, it was my first trip above the equator! I had no network at all, but I knew that I had an exciting product that had a track record in Australia, New Zealand and Singapore. It was a product especially designed for entrepreneurs, so the first thing I did was to start searching for the existing KPIs in London who were focused on serving entrepreneurs.

Through a friend of a friend, the first people I met with were already running an online entrepreneurs network with over 100,000 members in the UK. They loved the product I was launching and said they were happy to partner with me. The CEO suggested that I host a dinner party for about forty Key People of Influence in London who were focused on entrepreneurship.

The dinner party was a great success. I stood up and delivered my pitch; I then gave printed materials and product samples to everyone. It cost about $2,500 and ended up generating several great meetings which turned into partnerships. In the first week we launched, over 800 people attended our events and we made over $160,000 in sales. Rather than running expensive advertising campaigns, we focused on engaging with Key People of Influence and creating win/win partnerships. It resulted in a very lucrative start to doing business in London.

Your success will take a leap after a game-changing partnership. In the context of a great partnership, almost anything is possible.

## The spirit of partnership

When I think about partnerships, it starts with the right spirit of intent. You can't fake it when it comes to a successful partnership; you genuinely have to care about the wants and desires of the person you're doing the deal with. You need to see it from their side of the table and work as hard for them as you want them to work for you; or even more so.

This starts with your internal team of people who work with you every day. The spirit of partnership has to begin at the core of your business with the co-founders, the employees and the suppliers. Even the way you view those around you sets the tone for partnership. Larry Page describes the Google employees as the "team." He uses that word because he genuinely recognizes that he is only able to achieve his goals through partnering with other geniuses who decide to work at his company.

Beyond the internal team, the external relationships also thrive when there's a spirit of partnership. Your customers and clients are in partnership with your business in a way – they want a result and you want their business – if you focus on their needs they will take care of yours.

Your investor relationships will only last if you see them as your partners. Their money is allowing you to speed up your growth and your operation is providing them with a return on capital. It can be easy for an entrepreneur to forget how important that first investment was after the business is making big profits and investors sometimes forget that they were the ones who backed your long term plan. With the spirit of partnership, the relationship works.

Don't try to squeeze every drop out of a relationship. Allow others to have their triumphs, celebrate the wins of others even if it's not yet your turn. All of it comes down to being a good partner and being a good partner ensures you are a Key Person of Influence for the long run.

## The tools

Without the spirit of partnership, the tools are fairly useless, but provided you're creating win/win relationships you'll need a few ways to manage them.

### 1. Negotiations

It's worthwhile to learn the art and science of negotiations. The way you present a deal has a huge impact on the way it is received. The wording you use, the meeting place, the materials you bring and the way you follow up all impact the quality of the partnerships you form.

I do not believe you should use negotiation tactics to create unfair agreements; they simply won't last. I do believe that you should approach all negotiations in a professional way so that you reach an outcome everyone involved can be happy with. Good negotiations never involve manipulation; good negotiation skills revolve around your ability to see the full picture from both sides of the negotiation. It requires both parties to make sacrifices for the good of the partnership long-term.

## 2. Written agreements

Key People of Influence often attract many partners and a lot is discussed. In the spirit of good partnership, it's worth making sure that you keep a written agreement of any partnerships you create. This could be an employment contract, it could be an email confirmation, a Memorandum of Understand (MOU) or a fully developed contract put together by a law firm. Regardless of the way you choose to document the agreement, do it for the best interests of everyone involved, not so you can enforce a carefully concealed clause.

## 3. Systems

There are systems that track where every sale came from and pay a commission to the person who helped generate that sale. These are perfect for scaling marketing and referral agreements.

There are systems that measure how much time each contractor, supplier or employee put into a project. There are systems for managing a crowd funded shareholding with multiple investors.

Without these systems, you simply can't scale your partnerships. You want to invest in systems that allow you to have clear, clean relationships with people all over the world.

## What kind of deals can you start with?

There's several types of deals that I recommend you make as you build your skills as a Key Person of Influence.

## Affiliate partnerships

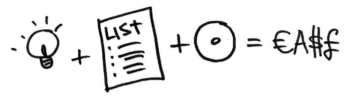

This is a partnership that encourages people to promote your products in exchange for a commission. The system uses tracking codes and links to report where every sale originated from and with the right software you can manage thousands of affiliates, who all promote you, and promptly receive a commission when they generate a sale. It's not a new concept (professionals have been paying finder's fees for years), but with modern technology you can really ramp it up.

Imagine you launch a web site selling t-shirts for $25. The front of the site is a normal-looking store; however, there's also a back end portal for affiliates. When an affiliate logs into the site, they are given a special link. They are told that anyone who arrives at the site through this link, and buys a t-shirt, will be logged as their affiliate sale and a commission of twenty percent will be paid. As an affiliate they are free to use email, Twitter, Facebook, blogs or videos to promote your site. The more people who click the link and buy a t-shirt, the more money they make for themselves and for you. The power of this system is that you don't spend your marketing money until after the sale is made.

We run Key Person of Influence events around the world and rather than spending a fortune on advertising up front, we engage with local supporters and run a grass-roots affiliate campaign. After we've run the event the commissions are paid or rewards are issued. You can register your interest in being an affiliate by emailing *affiliates@entrevo.com*.

## Co-promotion

This is when two companies with similar sized databases each mail their contacts about the other's offer. Sometimes the lists aren't exactly the same size, so you need to agree on how you will get around this. One company might add some money into the deal or mail their list several times to make up the difference. You will quickly discover that some of the people who never respond to your offers are suddenly interested in the new product you offer as part of the mail swap. I have had people tell me that they have a list that doesn't respond to anything, but when they mail this so-called "dead-list" with our offer, we soon find out that there's thousands of dollars' worth of new business.

## Product creation partnerships

This is where you team up with another person or a group to create a more valuable new product. Imagine a personal trainer teams up with an image consultant and a photographer to create a "Complete Makeover" package. It's a great way for all three businesses to work together and help the client to get the best result possible. Always approach this with the question, "what is my client trying to accomplish when they work with me and who could I team up with to get an even better outcome?"

In the above example, the client isn't looking to lift heavy plates of metal, spend money on clothes or sit around smiling at a cameraman. They want to tone-up, look fashionable and get some great photos while they are looking their best. By thinking about how you can help your client get something done, you will be able to identify who can help you to help your client.

## Packaging up

This is very similar to Product Teaming, except you are looking to add someone else's existing products to your own existing products. Imagine you are a restaurant and you are next to a cinema. You could do a "Movie-Meal Deal" and capture more customers and extra revenue. Think about the existing products and services that would complement your own product nicely and create a bundle.

## Free-bundle group

Everyone likes free stuff. Even better, they love bundles of free stuff. Why not team up with several businesses to put together an irresistible "basket of free goodies."

Let's imagine that you have a free meditation CD that you give to potential clients, while the yoga studio down the road gives away a free first lesson and a chiropractor friend gives away a free spine assessment. If you do a JV, each of you now has a very nice free offer you can use to attract new business and promote each other's businesses. How easy would it be to generate new leads if you created a free-bundle worth hundreds?

## Getting started with partnerships

All the time I hear people say, "I just had a good idea, but how do I actually make it happen?."

First, you should never ask, "*How* do I make it happen?"

You should ask, "*Who* do I need to talk to?"

Whenever you have an idea, no matter how crazy, make at least three calls to see if it's doable. Making three calls can yield you some amazing results.

My first real business was running underage dance parties with my best friend when we were just eighteen years old. In a bold move, I called the number one nightclub in town and told them we wanted to run a dance party for teens during the school holiday. I asked if they would meet with us to discuss a potential joint venture. They agreed to see us and we put forward a deal that made sure they would cover their costs with no risk and get lots of positive PR. They signed a deal on the spot.

Next we went to the local radio station and asked them to partner with us, too. They agreed that in exchange for sponsorship rights, they would give us free radio advertising. Six weeks later we ran the biggest teen dance party in the area that year and walked away with more cash than we could carry!

I learned a very valuable lesson. Whenever I have an idea now, I always pick up the phone and make three calls just to see what might happen. I am always surprised at how much can happen as a result of just three calls.

When Kevin Harrington was presented with an innovative new music system, he picked up the phone and called 50 Cent. The famous rapper agreed to get involved and appeared on TV with Kevin soon after. As a result, the product made sales of over twenty million dollars in its first few months!

You'll be surprised what happens when you jump on the phone and call three people who could really ramp things up; especially when you have a powerful pitch.

## Go networking for partnerships... Not clients

One of the key differences between Key People of Influence and everyone else is that KPIs don't go out looking for clients, they go looking for partnerships. Going out to a networking event looking for a client is like trying to get to China on foot. If you want to go to China, you don't want to go one step at a time, you want to figure out who already flies there in a jet. KPIs only go networking to find leverage. They are looking for people who have a big database of clients, a channel of distribution, a great brand, money to invest, an awesome product or some other key aspect of value or leverage.

I often get frustrated when people come up to me at a networking function and try to get me to become a client. I almost always like it when someone is thinking about a mutually beneficial partnership.

To step things up as a Key Person of Influence, forget looking for clients and start looking for relationships that can benefit both parties. Instead, ask:

- Do they have a list of potential clients?
- Are they interested in co-producing a product?
- Have they got a product that would be attractive to your contact list?
- Would this person be a valuable addition to the team?
- Is there a beneficial contact you can put them in touch with?

These are all powerful questions that yield better results than, "Can I make a sale right here and now?"

The money is in great partnerships. Whenever you want to take your income up to a higher level, go looking for a higher level partnership. A radical idea becomes fairly plausible when you have the right partners. If someone says they want to attract 100,000 customers, you'd probably have some doubts. If they then explain that they have partnerships with major media companies, celebrities, retail outlets and investors, you might start to think, "Only 100,000? Why so few?" Not much happens when you work in isolation; however, with the right partners, anything is possible.

## Meeting a potential partner

It can be nerve racking sitting down with someone who has the power to double your quarterly sales with a single email. You want to make sure you get a few things right so that the deal goes ahead and the relationship is long lasting.

## Set the scene

Meet people in a nice restaurant, hotel, club or lounge. In most cases it's best not to meet people in your office or theirs because the spirit of a JV should be about meeting on common ground to create a win/win/win deal (you win, I win, the customer wins). It can create the wrong starting point if one person has to make the trip to the other person's office. I also like meeting in nice locations because a JV or partnership should be about creating wealth and abundance for everyone involved.

## Bring a gift

When you meet with a potential partner, you might like to bring a thoughtful gift to show that you are thinking of their needs. It could be a copy of a book (yours perhaps). It could be something simple like a magazine article clipping you think they might be interested in. It's not to demonstrate that you're spending a lot of money on them; it's to demonstrate that you are already thinking about their interests.

## Make friends first

A deal will not normally happen if you don't like each other, even if the deal is perfect in every other way. Conversely, if you do like each other you will find it easy to make a deal work.

Kevin normally talks about anything other than business until he is sure he likes the person he's talking to. He genuinely wants to do business with people he likes and shares common ground with. If there's no "click-factor" Kevin normally won't make a deal even if everything else seems good.

## Do business last

When you have built rapport and it seems entirely appropriate to bring up business, it should only take twenty to thirty minutes to make a deal work. Much longer than that and it might not be a good deal to be doing. Always go into a meeting with a fair deal in mind and know in advance what you are flexible on and where you can't budge.

## Pick up the bill

I am personally a fan of genuinely offering to pick up the bill; especially if I instigated the meeting. For me it shows that I valued the meeting with them. Of course, if they insist on splitting the bill, I am okay with it, because it shows we are both thinking fifty-fifty even on small things.

## Follow through

After a meeting, allow fifteen minutes to follow through on anything you mentioned you would do. Sometime in the course of conversation you might say that you will email through a web site address, a name of a book or connect two people on email. Very few people actually follow through on these off-hand remarks, but it gets noticed when you do follow through and it sends a powerful message that what you say and what you do are the same thing.

## Expect magic

The most rewarding part of building a business with the spirit of partnership in everything you do is the unexpected rewards that show up. You know you've built solid partnerships when you're constantly surprised by how things turn out better than you expected.

Great partnerships have allowed me to make progress in ways I would have never imagined. As a result of partnerships, I've seen my businesses go global, I've received investment at the valuation I wanted, I have earned a high income, I've been given shares in growth companies, I have had a lot of fun, been invited on unique trips away and met my entrepreneurial heroes. None of these things would have happened if I hadn't built strong relationships that turned into strong partnerships.

# Exercises

What three calls can you make right now?

- Three people who already have a list?
- Three businesses that give away free stuff for your bundle?
- Three people who you can team up with and make a product?

What three calls could you make (regardless of how scary) that could really get your ideas off the ground?

Go for it!

## ACTION STEP

For additional content relating to this step visit:
*www.keypersonofinfluence.com/partnerships*

## Notes ...

## Hitting these five bases

What we've shared with you may seem simple. Kevin and I have given you just five things to focus on; however, never underestimate the power of simplicity. Built into these five outcomes for becoming a Key Person of Influence you will find that there is clarity, credibility, visibility, scalability and profitability.

Over the next twelve months, I can guarantee you that our email inboxes will be full of people emailing us their success stories, as a result of following the KPI Method. I already know what they will say. Their email will tell us that they did the work, pushed through their limiting beliefs, made the time and did all five of the steps in order (it's very important that you do the steps in order). They will then tell us that just as we promised, opportunities started to come their way, more money began to flow and they started to have more fun. They will tell us that they experienced three big benefits after doing the work set out in this book:

1. They earn more money with less stress and struggle.

2. They enjoy greater status and recognition in their industry and have more fun.

3. They attract more opportunities that are right for them.

I sincerely want *you* to be in that group. I want your story in our inbox, telling me that you have done these five simple things, made yourself an opportunity magnet, earned more money, had more fun and created more success. Sadly, there's a good chance you won't be. People can get addicted to the struggle and let complexity get in the way of simplicity; the unimportant stuff replaces the most important stuff, or worse, the desire for immediate quick wins creeps in.

In the next few chapters, we will share with you some of the things we've noticed when watching highly successful people make decisions versus people who are perpetually going around in circles. The next chapters will offer ideas on how you can overcome the obstacles and become the Key Person of Influence in your chosen field faster and without so many struggles.

# ③

# MAKING IT HAPPEN

*Our daily routines, habits and traditional education have gotten us this far, however now they are holding us back. We need to overcome the obstacles that get in the way of becoming a Key Person of Influence. It is not enough to know the path; we must walk it.*

## Newcomers, Worker-Bees and KPIs

There's a predictable journey you'll go on as you pursue success, achievement and influence. Every industry has three layers of people – Newcomers, Worker-Bees, and Key People of Influence.

The newcomers are enthusiastic, excited and full of dreams. They believe that this new industry they are in will fulfill their dreams and take them places. Newcomers are normally willing to work hard for little pay in the short term in the belief that the rewards will come later. Typically they have seen the results that a KPI has achieved and they want to replicate similar success for themselves.

The worker-bees are the people in the industry who are doing the work, but not getting ahead. Some of their previous dreams have been knocked out of them. When they were a newcomer, they thought that their industry would be fresh, new, exciting and rewarding. Now it seems a bit stale and they are secretly resentful of the Key People of Influence (for their effortless results) and the newcomers (for their spark and enthusiasm). The worker-bees at some point may have enjoyed the work, but are often disappointed that the results aren't coming in fast enough.

As we now know, the Key People of Influence make it look easy. They always have lots of opportunity flowing around them and they achieve great results quickly. Their email inbox is full of people trying to get good opportunities to them. With a few phone calls they can make magic happen and get some of the spoils. They also attract lots of newcomers into their industry because they make success seem so easy.

## The merry-go-round of distraction

This dynamic causes a strange phenomenon. Jaded worker-bees go buzzing about new industries and they spy a Key Person of Influence in that new area. They get excited and decide to become a newcomer to that industry. They feel the rush and excitement that comes with a brand new project. They see how effortless success comes to the KPIs in that industry. Even if a worker-bee enjoyed their previous job, they think to themselves, "I like what I do, but I don't get the rewards. So if I can make easy money in this new field, I can always go back to what I do and not worry about the money." Like most newcomers, they get energized and do lots of work for little rewards. They expect that this time the work will pay off in the long run.

After a while, the newcomer gets a bit tired and their new job starts to feel like hard work with less of the spark. They have now met a lot of worker-bees in this new industry who say things like

> *"It's hard work in this industry; I've been at it for years and I still haven't seen the big rewards yet."*

The newcomer becomes a worker-bee and begins looking around for the next big thing that will provide an easy win. As this continues, they get further and further from pursuing their passion by constantly chasing the next easy win. This opportunistic behavior is the very thing that prevents opportunities from flowing.

The answer to this conundrum is simple. You must focus on your passion and become a Key Person of Influence in that field. As soon as you are a KPI, you will not even notice opportunities in other industries because you will be swamped with great things to do in your own industry, and the rewards will come thick and fast.

There's no easy money, no quick wins, and no big payoff for newcomers or worker-bees – not in property, not in shares, not on the internet, not in a franchise, not in a network marketing business, not in technology, software, foreign exchange, wearables, apps or ecommerce. Easy wins go to Key People of Influence. Period.

Resist the temptation to chase the new thing and keep taking steps closer to the inner circle of the industry you love. Stop looking elsewhere and focus on implementing the KPI Method. When you focus on the five steps in this book and arrive as a Key Person of Influence, you will get to be the "overnight success" others are talking about.

## Hijack your habits

This isn't to say you can't learn from other industries. Kevin Harrington has a great saying, "Hijack your habits." He believes that observing other industries is a powerful way to gain a fresh approach.

One of Kevin's biggest deals came from exploring another industry. He booked a ticket to the Cannes Film Festival in France and rubbed shoulders with the big-wigs in the film industry. He learned that the typical Hollywood film makes more money through international distribution than the domestic US market. With that idea, he set about doing a deal to take his infomercial business into Europe using the same sort of strategies he saw in the film industry. He was able to make a deal with Rupert Murdoch and his company jumped from 100 million dollars in sales to over 500 million dollars as a result!

Most people see something exciting happening in another industry and they decide to jump ship and become a newbie in that field. A better plan is to observe the strategy in another market and apply the fresh approach to what you know.

## Achieving freedom

I often get asked the question, "If I become a Key Person of Influence, won't that mean I will be trapped in my business and I won't ever be able to sell it?"

It seems logical that a person who has a profile and is seen to be the driving force of a business would be trapped in the business, but in practical terms nothing is further from the truth. Key People of Influence are freer for several reasons.

First, they attract talent. Highly skilled and talented people don't want to work with just anyone; they want to work with KPIs. When you position yourself as a KPI, you'll start to see brilliant people who show up and make remarkable things happen. These people will be autonomous, value focused people who start to grow your business in all directions whether you're in the room or not. Pretty soon you'll have so much talent buzzing around your enterprise that there will seem to be a steady stream of savvy people always showing up. This is called "high performance culture," and it's a big asset whether you want to sell your business one day or hand over the day-to-day management to a leader who's better suited to the task than yourself.

Secondly, people who are KPIs have created assets that deliver value when they aren't even in the room. Donald Trump can be flying about in his private jet and still be having an impact on thousands of people worldwide. He does this through his brand, his books and TV shows, his products and services, and his profile and partnerships. On your own scale, you'll be doing this too. As a KPI, even when you're not in the room, your presence is felt.

Third, Key People of Influence attract investors far more than worker-bees do. An investor wants to put their money behind the person who's leading the way and going places. A Key Person of Influence can show all the signs that they are worthy of receiving these funds. If there is an exit whereby someone wants to buy the whole company, there are still dozens of ways you can transfer your brand value to the new owner.

The truth is, nothing is more restrictive than being average and ordinary. The worker bees in any industry aren't able to get traction or attraction for their ideas. There's no point trying to hide out behind your business or website anymore. Even if you do build a small business, the moment you try to compete with a KPI, they will snap up all your clients at speed. These days, systems are freely available, generic products can be copied and business brands seem to blend into the sea of sameness; what really stands out is a story, a personality and a person who really cares. Being a Key Person of Influence will set you free. Hiding out is a recipe for going nowhere.

## You can't do it alone

There's no such thing as a self-made millionaire; success is always a team sport.

In the previous chapter we explored the leverage that comes from partnering with others. It saves you years and a lot of money when you find the right people to work with.

It doesn't end there. There's leverage that comes from learning from people who have the results you want. There's leverage that comes from surrounding yourself with a peer group who are achieving at a high level. There's leverage that comes from sharing your journey as a Key Person of Influence.

I am always surprised when someone tries to do something on their own; I'm convinced that some people want to create an "original mistake." In these globally-connected times, it's possible to find someone who has done what you want to achieve already and learn from them. Creating a book or a product could potentially be difficult, time consuming and expensive. You might be too close to your own material to spot its real value. Why would you risk your time, energy and money trying to create something without the right support?

When left alone, most people become distracted, bored, discouraged and uninspired; they will not complete any of the KPI Method outcomes to their full potential. It's almost a cliché that people are "working on a book" and can let countless hours of great content slip through their fingers. You may have already done this.

Consider that every talk you have given could have been a podcast, that every meeting could have been an interview for your book. The truth is we will never achieve our full potential on our own. That's why every great sports person has a coach; that's why the president has advisors and why great actors have a director to bring out their best.

It's encouraging having someone to push you and bring out your best work. Right now, I am writing on a deadline and I have someone keeping me accountable. I also have people who I respect and admire who will read the draft, so I am pushing myself to perform.

## The power of current best-practices

Unfortunately, most people who attempt to hit these targets on their own make costly mistakes. They procrastinate and waste time and too often they create an inferior product that fails to create the desired outcome. It may even damage their brand rather than build it. It is disappointing to see someone on video who has nothing unique to say. They talk in general terms and create no gravity to their ideas. They were given the gift of having a captive audience and blew it with amateur efforts.

The other important point to remember is that whatever you put online is potentially there for life. Getting it wrong can leave you with content that keeps coming back to haunt you.

Without the right guidance, people over-commit to needless expenses (like high-cost printing, design, filming, etc.) They spend their time and money in the wrong area. Nothing really links back to their business model and it all looks a little sad. People do this because they are unaware of current best-practices. In every industry there are cutting edge strategies and methods that form the basis of current best-practices; and these practices evolve over time.

When I started in business, a best-practice for my industry was to market my business on the right-hand column of the newspaper; today the best-practices relate to online advertising and content marketing strategies. In a few years from now, things will change again. For this reason, it's essential to be part of a group that talks about these issues and is committed to staying close to the current best practices.

## Leveraging experts

The world we live in has shrunk. Almost anyone on the planet can be reached and learned from. Experts are available to help you to implement best-practices and apply them to your specific outcome.

Many people who struggle in business hate paying for help. They try to do it all themselves; they struggle to build their own website, design their own brochures, enter their expense accounts and devise their own marketing plans. That's not how the pros do it. People who are high-achievers ensure they are surrounded by experts who can help them to implement their vision. They don't risk making painful mistakes that someone else has already made. There are people who have achieved the goals you have set for yourself and they can help you get there faster, cheaper and at a higher standard.

For every project Kevin gets involved in, he surrounds himself with the Key People of Influence in that field. He uses top consultants, lawyers, accountants and advisors. He's surrounded with people who help build his business. Even with all his experience, if Kevin is working on a pitch, he wants to work on it with a team whose pitches have made millions in profit. If he's launching a new product, he wants to work with people who have created hot products that sell globally for a profit. He sees success as a team sport.

Give yourself the gift of leveraging the success of others. Make sure you get support and guidance from people with results on your journey to become the Key Person of Influence in your industry.

## The illusion of limited resources

Beware of the "Illusion of Limited Resources" because this mindset will hold you back in every area of business. Professor Paul Zane Pilzer, a senior economic advisor and internationally acclaimed author, says that a resource is only defined by our ability to use it. Effectively, there are no resources without *resourcefulness*. The only reason oil is a resource, is because humans are resourceful enough to use it for so many things. Before we understood it, it was nothing more than black sludge.

There's a good chance you are already standing on an oil well of opportunities that are just waiting for you to become resourceful enough to see them. If you don't believe me, try to imagine what would happen if tomorrow morning Kevin Harrington swapped lives with you for a year. He would get your house, your car, your friends, your family, your challenges and even your bank account. Imagine that he would even have to take on your name and appearance. In twelve months, when you swap back, do you think there would be some noticeable changes in your life?

Of course there would! He would spot opportunities that you had overlooked. He would pick up the phone and have conversations that you would not have had. He would start to introduce himself more powerfully than you currently do. What about poor Kevin when he has to go back to his life in twelve months. If you hadn't been as resourceful as him, he might find that his houses and cars have been repossessed!

We all want a billionaire's resources, but very few people are willing to get even a little bit more resourceful than they currently are. After reading this book, I sincerely hope you are willing to stretch and do what it takes to become the Key Person of Influence in your industry. No matter what you need in your business or your life, getting it will be a function of your resourcefulness rather than whether the resources are available. Of course they are available.

## The three biggest factors that determine your resourcefulness are:

1. The questions you ask.
2. The people you know.
3. Your willingness to stretch into the unknown.

Let's take a look at these three factors in the next section.

## Better answers come from better questions

If ever I hear myself complaining about not having access to enough resources, I know I need to look at the questions I'm asking myself. If I've been complaining, the chances are that I've been asking *unresourceful questions* like:

"How come I can't find the time?"

"Why is this so hard?"

"Why can't there just be an easier way?"

"Why do I have to do this? Why can't someone else do it?"

I know straight away that I need to ask a better question, and immediately, if I do ask a better question, I will get a better answer.

Here are some *better* questions:

"Who would absolutely love the chance to work on this project and would be able to do an amazing job?"

"What value can I add to this, that very few people could?"

"How do I make this even better?"

"Who has already achieved the result I want?"

"Who woke up this morning and already has access to the resources I want?"

There's no point complaining and there's no point asking questions that go nowhere. What's a better question you need to ask yourself now?

## Requests vs. Opportunities

By the very fact that you want to grow your business or your levels of influence, you'll need to access resources. Many people focus on the resources they are lacking and aren't shy about telling everyone. They attempt to make their problems into someone else's problems. You hear some people say things like:

"I need more sales coming in. Can you help me make more sales?"

"I need my team to get motivated. Can you get me a motivated team?"

"I want more qualified leads. Can someone get me some better leads please?"

"I want my suppliers to give me a better deal. Can I get a better deal from suppliers?"

All of these are just requests. Unless you are a child asking your parents for something small, the language of requests does not work very often. Key People of Influence use the language of opportunities. This is where you win by helping someone else win. When you want something, you express it in a way that works for the person you want assistance from.

Here are some examples:

"I need more sales coming in. Would you like to follow up on some hot leads and get ten percent of the money you bring in?"

"I need my team to get motivated. If I could see an improvement in performance, I would happily share some of the upside with you. What kind of conditions would make that deal a win for you?"

"I want more qualified leads. If we can get more targeted leads, we will save a lot of wasted time and money. I would be happy to share some of those savings with you. Would you like to get involved in that project?"

"I want a better deal on supplies. If I ordered in bulk, would you be able to offer me better terms?"

Great business people speak the language of opportunity *all* the time. In the next week, see if you can eradicate requests from your language and adopt a policy that you only offer opportunities. You'll be astonished at how many people will get excited to work with you when there's an opportunity on the table as opposed to a request.

## It's not just what you know

Some people go to networking functions and collect business cards. They look at them proudly and think, "Look at how big my network is." In truth though, they don't have a network, they have a pile of business cards. A network is a group of people who share opportunities. You can pick up the phone to them, they happily take your call and they trust that you will have something valuable to say.

If you think of your network in those terms, how many people do you have in your directory that fit the criteria? How many people do you regularly share opportunities with? If the number is low, you need to make this a major priority. You will never sustainably increase your wealth without first increasing your network. As a Key Person of Influence, this will be much easier than you think. People love being able to take a call from a person who is clear about the game they are playing, who's credible, valuable and renowned for something.

With these things in place, the quality of your network will develop at pace, but there's even more that can be done to ramp things up. First, get in the habit of spotting great opportunities for others. Quite often, I will see something in a blog and email it to a friend. Quite often, I will connect two people who I know can do business together. Quite often, I will share an idea with someone if I think it would be beneficial. I don't spot opportunities for friends because I am looking for an immediate reward. I do it because I believe that it strengthens my network. Given time, a strong network leads to more wealth, more fun and more success.

## The best time to start your dream is now

It may be human nature to wait until you feel that you have all your ducks in a row to start your new venture. But waiting is not only the hardest part; it could turn out to be your worst course of action. During the course of Kevin's thirty years in direct response marketing, he came to the realization that the best time to put an idea into action is *now*. Sometimes you just don't know what will happen until you try.

Passion plays a tremendous role in any endeavor – whether you're formulating a business plan for a new restaurant or the Snuggie blanket. You must overcome any fear or apprehension you may have. Know in your heart that if you've chosen the right partners and mentors – and you believe in yourself and your product – the time to act really is right now.

While working as an investor on the original *Shark Tank* TV show, my advice was to forget about the people and the cameras, and believe in yourself, your product and what you can do for others. Channel your excitement and your belief in yourself. Practice. Then practice some more.

Kevin's favorite quote is from Paul J. Meyer:

> *"Whatever you vividly imagine, ardently desire, sincerely believe and enthusiastically act upon must inevitably come to pass."*

Upon waking each morning, recite that quote. Make it your mantra too. Tell yourself in no uncertain terms that success is going to happen. That's how Kevin overcame his fear, and that's how he lives his life.

We're not saying you are going to hit a home run every time out of the box. What we're saying is that until you launch your plan or product you have zero chance at success. Sure, there will be times when you need to pull back to reboot or tweak your venture, but eventually, believing it and acting upon it makes it happen.

Kevin is always on the lookout for, "The next Snuggie." So too are other investors. If they don't know about your idea or invention, they can't act upon it.

You can analyze and plan as thoroughly as possible, but you'll never make a dime on a product that doesn't hit the market. Never allow yourself to get discouraged by challenging situations. Instead, step back and find a way around them! There's no time like the present to launch your idea – the one you've felt so passionately about for so long.

This is your dream we're talking about here. It's your passion. And possibly even your life's purpose. Take your dream, wake up and make it happen.

## Stretching into the unknown

Most people believe that when the conditions are right they will act. This attitude does *not* work. Ever. It's like saying that when all the lights turn green, I will leave my house and drive to work. Not only do the conditions never become perfect for action, but most people wouldn't act even if they were. Most people have become so used to not committing to things that when the time comes for them to act, they just don't do anything.

After witnessing many successful people and many of those who struggle, I can tell you that the people who are successful are the ones who commit to things that take them forward, even when they aren't sure exactly how it will all come together. I'm not saying be reckless, I'm just saying that there's never a right time. You will *always* have challenges going on with your time, your money or your focus. If something comes along that you know you should do, then do it, and figure it out along the way.

## Ready, Fire... Aim!

Here's an example in your hands: this book was written at a time that was incredibly busy for me. If I decided that in order for me to write this book I would wait until I had a spare three to four weeks, it would have never happened. Instead, I just started writing it and I committed to write a thousand words a day no matter what.

I have written it on planes, in hotels, and at all hours of the day and night. I even wrote until four in the morning, knowing that I would need to be up at 9.30 a.m. It was difficult to get out of bed, sure, but after a shower I was fine, and I made up the sleep later that afternoon.

When I was twenty-four, I wanted to buy myself a BMW X5 with all the extras. Despite knowing exactly what I wanted, I put off the decision for over a year. Then one day, a friendly rival of mine bought himself a new BMW. The next day I went down to the finance department and signed up for the lease on the car, not knowing exactly how long I could afford to make my payments.

After the lease was approved, it just became another thing I needed to find the money for each month, and sure enough, I did it. There's no way I would have ever had that car if I had waited until I had "spare" money lying around. That car was a huge source of fun and achievement; to this day I'm really glad I acted first then figured it out.

Elon Musk was in massive debt and at risk of losing everything because of his ambitious dream to launch a rocket more efficiently than NASA. Even in his darkest hours, he just kept moving forward and committed himself to the outcome. Somehow he figured it all out, because he had to. Currently, he's building electric cars at Tesla, distributing solar panels at Solar City and launching reusable rockets at SpaceX. He acts first, then he figures it out because he must.

I wish the universe worked differently. I wish that you could plan to do things and then magically make time and money to then do them. It would feel a lot safer. But unfortunately, I don't see that happening for anyone I know. The people I know over-commit themselves then figure it all out as it unfolds.

Earlier, I said:

*"Resources show up after Resourcefulness."*

The more resourceful you are, the more resources you will have. That's true, but here's the secret that few people share:

*"Resourcefulness shows up after you make a commitment."*
#kpibook

Prior to committing to something, half of your resourcefulness is working on overtime on why this is *not* a good idea." Without a commitment, humans use up too much brain energy on assessment of the idea, the timing and trying to predict an unpredictable future. When you finally commit to an outcome, you free up gallons of energy to become more resourceful in following through. Commit to a big goal (I mean literally sign yourself up to some sort of deadline or external commitment) and then start filling in the blanks.

## Don't wait for the ideal time

Becoming a Key Person of Influence doesn't happen for most people because they are waiting for "the ideal time." They think that "one day" they will have the time, money and focus to get something done. So they keep working towards making enough money or earning enough vacation days rather than going for what they want. I ask them, "Why are you working so hard?" They reply, "So I can get some spare time and money to go and do what I want."

No, no, no, no! Don't work to make money for the ideal time, work for the result. Ask yourself what it is you actually want to do. Then go and do it.

There is no ideal time. It never comes. You will be an elderly person in an aged care home and finally you will realize that had you just gone for what you wanted, you would have had it. An "ideal time" is not a goal. Bite off more than you can chew and then figure it out as you go. If you were any good at creating an ideal time in your life, you would have had one by now. When was the last time you actually arrived at the perfect time and place with all the money you needed. It's a fairytale.

If you suddenly realize that the most important thing you could be doing for your success is to write a book, then don't put it off. If you know in your heart of hearts that you should be starting a business, then go start it. If it's time to sell your business, then sell it.

I'm not saying that you should be reckless; I'm just saying when something is important, you should begin it now rather than waiting for all the circumstances to be perfect. There's never enough time, there's never enough money, there's never a perfect plan. That's life. Move forward anyway.

If you are wrong about your idea, very rarely is the downside catastrophic. In past civilizations, people who had bad ideas died. They were eaten by bears, burned at the stake, tortured to death, or worse. Today, the absolute worst thing that most people fear is the feeling of being a labeled a failure. Many people's worst nightmare is getting embarrassed because their idea didn't work out the way they thought it would. At worst, they may lose some time and start-up capital.

Imagine trying to explain that to your ancestors! Your ancestors would shake their heads in disgust. They faced wars, plagues and disasters to create a better world and you're not taking full advantage of all it has to offer? You owe it to them to be braver and make some bold moves to achieve your dreams.

With the ideas in this book, the downside is *nothing!* I'm asking you to put some thought into your pitch, invest time to write, pluck up the confidence to produce some materials, use free tools on the internet and go out to speak with a few people. It will take some thought; it will take some time; and you might need to invest some money and get some guidance along the way, but if you commit to doing these things, you will jump to a whole new level. You have virtually no downside in perfecting your pitch, writing your book, producing a product, using social media and talking to some people about a partnership.

The upside, however, is *awesome*.

## Eight ways to reignite your passion for success

No matter what or who you're involved in, it's tough to keep the fires of passion burning. Even the world's best singers get bored with their own songs from time to time.

You can lose your passion because the results aren't showing up fast enough or simply because success requires some repetition once you have a winning formula. But you can't give up now. Not when you've lived and breathed your ideas for as long as you can remember.

So how do you retain the passion – or reignite it when you're tired, frustrated and maybe even broke? This may not help, but you need to remind yourself that we all get discouraged at some point. If you are feeling like your pilot light is out, don't let your dreams go down in flames. Here are a few ways to spark your excitement and stay the course.

**Take a break:** This may sound counter intuitive, but it really can do you and your passion a world of good to step away from your product or business plan for a few weeks – or maybe even a month. Your mind works in mysterious ways. It sometimes works better when you aren't consciously trying to break through a plateau or obstacle.

**Study up:** Hit the Internet and do some research into how others have succeeded after encountering similar frustrations. Watch a few videos of others who've enjoyed tremendous entrepreneurial success. Their excitement and joy is a great motivator. You'll want to dive right back into your work if you find the right inspiration.

**Find a mentor:** It's great having someone to turn to when things get rough, especially when that someone is a person who was once where you are now – someone who learned the secret to success and is willing to share it with you. The KPI Program is brilliant for mentoring and support. Visit: *www.keypersonofinfluence.com*

**Lower the bar:** If your idea of business success is launching a new product in six months and making your first million in three years, step back and adjust your numbers. Maybe it will take you a year to get that product off the ground and maybe you won't see a million dollars quite so soon. Giving yourself more time to get it right weakens your self-imposed myth that you are a failure at business because you didn't keep up with Mark Zuckerberg.

**Learn to delegate:** It's your dream and your team, but that doesn't mean you have to carry the ball on every play. Divvy up the duties among the members of your team. They'll feel empowered and more important – and you'll be able to focus on big-picture matters rather than the daily grind.

**Become more unsocial:** Put down your smart phone. Step away from your tablet. You'll feel less stressed and more focused if you don't try to answer all your emails or respond to all your texts immediately. Staying focused is really a key when you are trying to launch a product or fine-tune a business plan. Constant starts and stops are stressful and can leave you feeling unfulfilled after a long day's work.

**Befriend encouragers:** A super way to keep your entrepreneurial passion alive is to hang out with optimistic and encouraging individuals. Jettison the naysayers and cozy up to the "you can do it" crowd. Negative people are like energy vampires that can suck the life – and passion – out of you.

**Tune out from TV:** The news, the sitcoms, the movies and the infomercials are all designed to distract you. A lot of it is negative and it's easy to get caught up for hours every day. Tune out, sit quietly and let your mind wander rather than having the TV create more noise.

The bottom line is to do whatever you can to keep your passion or get it back. Work without passion is... well, work! The great thinkers and doers of the world have been fueled by their passion.

## What to look forward to next

Remember why you are becoming a Key Person of Influence. Remember what sparked this journey in the first place. Keep focused on your Big Game and why you want to win.

> *"When you are a Key Person of Influence you don't chase great opportunities, they come and find you."*
> #kpibook

Fame, recognition, financial windfall, passive income, and other exciting opportunities are commonplace for KPIs. These things are nearly impossible for people who are not yet a Key Person of Influence in their industry.

Here are some tangible things to expect once you are a KPI:

**Media and PR –** The media are always looking for expert opinions, feature stories and case studies. Once you are a KPI, start talking to the media and letting them know what you are up to. Send journalists your book with your bio. When they have a relevant story, they will think of you.

**Speaking at events** – One speaking opportunity can generate seriously valuable opportunities if done correctly. Remember that speaking opportunities go to KPIs not great speakers. By the time you have hit the five main outcomes set out in this book, speaking opportunities will have already started to find you.

**Directorships** – Many companies are willing to pay sizeable fees, or even equity, to have an established Key Person of Influence as a member of their board.

**Your own membership group** – As a KPI, you can put together a membership group. Either online or at a live venue, these groups can be a great source of income as well as a constant stream of opportunities. Start inviting people to come and join you. You will be amazed at how fast your group can grow.

**Subscribers** – As a KPI, you can easily have an inner circle of subscribers who pay for premium content or contact with you. I know several KPIs who make over six figures profit from their subscriber groups and their subscribers love them for it.

**Random surprises** – KPIs get invited on fun holidays, they get sent free gifts, they get invites to be VIP guests at events and many other fun surprises show up unannounced.

Be sure to keep your eyes on the prize. The reason you are doing this is because all the best opportunities go to KPIs. As a KPI, you will have more fun, make more money and enjoy more recognition. If you don't become a KPI, you will get stuck chasing revenue, spending too much time searching for (half decent) opportunities and forever feeling undervalued.

## Inertia and the power of momentum

You probably hated learning physics at school. You might remember thinking, "What a completely pointless subject," but the laws of physics are the same laws that govern your success.:

**Rule 1: The Law of Inertia** — An object at rest will stay at rest until acted upon by an outside force.

And its opposite:

**Rule 2: The Law of Momentum** — An object in motion will stay in motion until it meets a resisting force.

These two universal laws should remind you that when you feel the spark to do something, you should act on it straight away. Momentum is too precious to lose. It's a gift that comes far too scarcely.

If you feel compelled to act, then go for it. As you get going, you will find that you gather pace and produce an enormous amount of work. Often I am happy to sit up until three in the morning working on something, just so I don't break the momentum.

Of course if you don't act, you become governed by the law of inertia. You become an object at rest, destined to stay at rest until you get a big kick in the rear. Far too often, the outside force that gets you to eventually act comes in the form of pain. You realize that you haven't achieved any of your goals in two years. You lose a job. You lose a client. You lose a relationship. Inertia weighs you down and it takes more and more effort to get moving. Momentum is the feeling of being in flow. It's a rush and it's the domain of creativity.

Why are we telling you this?

Because if you have read this far, then deep down inside something is telling you that you are ready to establish yourself as a Key Person of Influence. You have an important pitch to share, you have an amazing book in you, you have a valuable product to produce and you have a worthy message to spread to the world. With those things in place, you will shine so brightly, that others will want to partner with you in sharing your value. It's time to stretch. It's time to invest your time, energy and money in doing these things. It won't be easy, but it will be worth it.

You've read this book for a reason and that reason is to act. You're here to do it, not to learn about it. Enough with the learning; now is your time to become the Key Person of Influence in your Industry.

# KPI: CASE STUDIES

## Lazo Freeman

When I first met Lazo Freeman, he told me he was a Personal Trainer. I wasn't surprised; he certainly looks the part. After chatting for a while, I discovered that he isn't just any Personal Trainer; he's actually a multi-award winning body builder. He's won major titles for Natural Body Building, and he even won a competition to meet Cindy Crawford!

What did surprise me was that despite his awards, his hourly rate was only marginally higher than my Personal Trainer, who had not won any awards. Lazo was charging about thirty percent higher than the industry average. Like many in his industry, he thought that the key to his success was completing more courses, getting more qualifications and having a nice brochure. Lazo was working hard with his clients, getting great results, but not seeing big financial rewards.

I started telling Lazo about my KPI Strategy and he instantly got it. He could see straight away that he hadn't differentiated himself from other personal trainers and that he hadn't yet used his success to establish himself as a KPI.

The first thing we did was to develop his pitch. Today, rather than introducing himself as a "Personal Trainer," Lazo will tell you he does, "Radical 12-week body transformations with highly successful people who do amazing things in their work, but very ordinary things naked." That line always gets a laugh, but more importantly, people want to see pictures of the twelve-week transformations.

When Lazo pulls out his book and shows them some before-and-after shots of his clients, jaws hit the floor. In twelve-weeks, Lazo can transform a skinny guy into a buff guy, or a fat man into a muscle man. The transformations are extraordinary.

He then directs them to his DVD and invites people to become friends with him on Facebook. By the time you see all of his photos, his YouTube videos and his testimonials, you know that he is *the* man for "radical twelve-week transformations in London."

Before you get too excited about getting him to work with you, I had better inform you of what happened to his prices. Today Lazo charges $15,000 for a Radical 12-Week Transformation, and he has a waiting list! This makes him the highest paid personal trainer in London.

It wasn't the awards that made it happen. It wasn't the four years of getting outstanding results with his clients. It was becoming a KPI caused such a huge shift. Lazo is now a KPI in his industry and is able to charge 500 percent of what the normal person in his industry charges. He earns more than most doctors or lawyers and he has a lot more fun, because he works in his passion.

## Mike Symes

When I first met Mike Symes, he was already successful. He had founded a marketing consultancy that specialized in assisting financial services companies. He wasn't short business, but still had to go looking for his new clients.

Mike wanted to take things up a level. He wanted to be priced in the premium end of the market (a well-justified position) and he wanted clients chasing him rather than the traditional method of pitching for new business.

Mike signed up to the KPI Program in April 2010 and immediately had a breakthrough in the way he explained the value he delivers to a client. Rather than saying, "I have a financial marketing agency," Mike began telling clients that he "works with financial services companies to ignite their brands, illuminate their points of difference and enable their messages to spread like wildfire, leaving them and their customers feeling inspired" (Pitch).

He then set to work on his book, *Find Your Firebrand*, in which he was able to consolidate his twenty-five years of industry experience into a powerful manuscript (KPI Step: Publish). In doing so, he was able to uncover and explore his unique Intellectual Property. Mike discovered that he had a lot more value to share than he had previously acknowledged.

Next, Mike produced a new web site and a highly valuable brand assessment tool which could allow people all over the world to access his unique take on Financial Services Branding (Product). With newfound clarity and scalability, Mike wasted no time in raising his profile online. This resulted in him being appointed as the Chairman of a highly prestigious industry body (Profile). Mike was also able to form joint ventures and partnerships with key industry players (Partnerships). With all of this in place, Mike noticed a clear shift in the amount of new business that was finding him. In one instance the CEO of one of the UK's largest banks was excited to have the opportunity to sit down over coffee with Mike to discuss the future of their brand.

In a six month period, Mike Symes went from being a very successful marketing consultant to a Key Person of Influence in his field. He went from being great at pitching for new business to having people pitch to him to become a client. Mike widened his scope to deliver value worldwide and distilled his unique ideas into valuable Intellectual Property. He recognized the mountain of value he was already standing on and is now producing at a whole new level.

Watch the video of Mike Symes sharing his KPI experience at: *www.keypersonofinfluence.com/successstories*

## Paul Fowler

Paul Fowler has spent a lifetime fascinated by flying. His earliest memories are of building cardboard wings and trying to take flight from the roof of the garden shed. As a teenager, he started parachuting and eventually joined the army as a paratrooper. Paul's passion then led him to become a pilot, where he spent years flying all over the world.

Even after being forced into an early retirement through illness, Paul still couldn't keep away from planes. He took himself down to the local flying club and started working there to try and rescue the club from bankruptcy. At the end of twelve months, Paul made a deal to buy the Oxfordshire Flying Club and flight school, and for the first time, he was a business owner with something he could get passionate about.

His health improved, as did the health of the flight school. Paul had begun to channel his lifetime passion into a business that had wings. Yet, despite his passion for the business, he hit a glass ceiling after the third year. The club grew popular with flying fanatics, but something was stopping it from growing to the size it needed to be to cover the bills and pay Paul a wage.

For the next two years, Paul struggled to figure out what would make his beloved flight school really get off the ground. He attended marketing boot camps, business networking events and pored over books on marketing and leadership. Nothing seemed to be working; the business was flying on one engine.

Then in mid-2010, Paul heard about the Key Person of Influence strategy. He had never even thought about the idea that he could make a name for himself in aviation. "The industry is so big. It employs millions of people. -I never dreamed I could become a Key Person or have any Influence; the idea never crossed my mind until I heard Daniel Priestley talking about it," says Paul.

After joining the program, his first step was to identify a micro-niche and learn how to make a pitch "I've always dreamed of owning a Spitfire aircraft and I guessed other people would want to fly one as well, so I decided to go for my lifetime dream and create the Spitfire Project," Paul says.

At the Perfect Pitch workshop, Paul developed his idea and arrived at a clear way to explain it to others. "Mike Harris told me to get out and start pitching it to see how people respond," says Paul. "He also said I should go looking for people who say that it will never work because they will help to identify where the pitch needs to be stronger."

As a result of pitching the idea to anyone who would listen, three months later Paul was crystal clear on his pitch. He then set about writing an article for the number one industry magazine, *Pilot*. He phoned the editor and pitched his article and the editor gave Paul a double-page spread dedicated to the Spitfire project on the spot, even before he had finished his pitch!

Within months, Paul was being invited to speak around the country about his project and gathering interested parties who wanted to invest in the iconic plane and take lessons to learn to fly it. Off the back of the article, Paul was approached by the BBC and a local TV station to discuss making a documentary on the project.

With so much buzz being created, Paul knew he needed to start focusing on productizing the business. He set about creating a "Zero to Hero" program that would fast track a private pilot from beginner level through to flying their own Spitfire. It was a bold move, but it received a lot of immediate interest. He also began putting his flight briefings onto audio and video so that people could learn from home and share their excitement with friends.

"It's funny; we do dozens of flight briefings each week, but until KPI I'd never even thought of them as potential products. I'm guessing most businesses are the same; they probably have more opportunities under their noses than they think."

Next, Paul worked to build an online social media profile for his flight school and his Spitfire Project. "I'm blown away at how many people are now reading our blogs and watching our videos on the web."

Finally, with all this in place, Paul was able to begin cultivating joint ventures and partnerships with other businesses in the industry. Some of his first deals involved having the flight school promoted to lists of over 10,000 people as well as a win/win partnership a local hotel.

"I now feel like I am on track to be a Key Person of Influence in my Industry. KPI gave me a map to follow and helped me to see where I was on the map. Then it gave me the strategy to move forward to where I wanted to be. My flight school is finally taking off and I'm feeling good about being in the captain's seat," says Paul.

## Jane Malyon

Jane Malyon is lovely and nice. Everyone says so because she has such a wonderful manner and warm disposition.

When we met Jane she had come from a thirty-year background in hospitality and catering, and had also been in business as a coach and trainer. Her niche was centered on resolving conflict, using your best etiquette under pressure and having better manners.

As Jane crafted her pitch, she began to realize she had a deep burning desire to bring the best out in people. Not just some people, but thousands of them. She wasn't sure how this would happen, but she knew something big was starting to stir.

Jane wrote the book, *Play Nicely*, and was forced to dive deep into her core ideas and philosophies on what makes people behave at their best and win people over with rapport and kindness, rather than by authority. During the KPI process, when Jane worked on her products, she hit a roadblock. She explored voicing a CD, creating a training program and even developing software. Nothing seemed to deliver the special experience she knew she wanted to create. Then, after randomly meeting an elderly lady who had become too frail to travel to the Savoy for her favorite annual treat of elegant afternoon tea, Jane had a flash of inspiration and imagined chilled delivery of a high-quality gift box containing ready to enjoy high-tea and scones.

It was perfect. For years, Jane had entertained family and friends at the Savoy or Ritz Carlton for afternoon tea and she was always delighted at the way her guests would naturally be at their best. The experience was natural, fun and filled with rapport – and the conversations encouraged collaboration and togetherness. It was everything she wanted to deliver to the world and it worked like magic!

To build her profile, Jane set an audacious goal to win a Guinness World Record. She called in all sorts of favors and remarkably set the world record for the largest gathering in one place, all enjoying English cream tea. She was featured on the BBC, newspapers, magazines, blogs and as a speaker at large conferences.

With the added profile, Jane noted that orders started to fly in and so did offers for partnership. People didn't just want to buy her product, they also wanted to license her brand! Within two years of launch, The English Cream Tea Company has shipped thousands of products all over the UK and built a brand that is set to expand globally. Jane's products are being used as gifts to say, "Thank you," "I'm sorry," and even as "a substitute for a hug," said one loyal customer.

This new business combines the best parts of Jane's story: catering, hospitality, coaching and a desire to bring out the best in people. Jane's vision of inspiring people to play nicely is fast becoming a reality!

See Jane telling her story *http://bit.ly/JaneMalyon*

## Darren Finkelstein

Darren and I stood eye-to-eye staring each other down across the table. He was arguing with me that the KPI method wouldn't work for him. Darren sells boats or at least that's what he was telling me at the time. He didn't believe that writing a book would make any difference and he didn't think it was possible to create any products.

After a short, sharp exchange, I said to him, "You're not in the boat sales business you're in the boat *ownership* business." He instantly got it. His business shouldn't be built around a single transaction his business should be built around the entire experience of owning a boat.

Darren co-founded his Melbourne based business because of his belief that "life is better with a boat," but after ten years in business, he had lost touch with the original intention of his business. After reconnecting with the "joy of boat ownership," Darren suddenly felt a flood of new energy and inspiration.

When people spoke to him, he started talking about all the fun his clients have on boats. He talked about how the kids put down the PlayStations and really connected with their parents on the boat. He talked about special boating adventures that people had and how many owners feel completely free when they're out at sea. He no longer pitches the sale; instead he talks from the heart about the experiences of a boat owner.

His book was written and published in just 200 days. *Honey, Let's Buy a Boat* is now selling copies all over the world and tells the full story of what owning a boat is all about. His book covers the purchase, the upkeep, the enjoyment and the sale or upgrade.

Darren has added almost a dozen new products and services to his business. Under the new umbrella of boat ownership, his company now services, refuels, restocks, washes and valet parks their clients' boats. They also teach people how to become better boat owners and have more enjoyment on the water. This has added an uplift to Darren's business that is unheard of in his industry.

After the release of his book, building a profile came easy. Darren was featured in the media and prominent magazines read by his market. He has spoken all over Australia to crowds of boat owners and he's become a trusted commentator in his industry. Most of this activity has ended up online and he's all over the front page of Google when you start searching for him or his business.

Darren loves growing his business through partnerships. He focuses on creating win/win alliances with others in the industry who are making life better with boats. Darren even turned down a major opportunity because it didn't feel like a true partnership that would go beyond a fast transaction. As Darren says, "If it's not good long term, it's not good short term."

Darren is in his zone now and looking at ways to grow his business. Rather than chasing the next sale, he's advancing the cause of enjoyable boat ownership. Darren and I catch up at least a few times a year and I always remind him of that conversation where he rediscovered his passion for boat ownership. After all, if you don't own a boat, it's wise to be friends with a guy who has a busy marina.

## Jacqui Sharples

Some people are pretty fit, but Jacqui Sharples is an athlete. She's a pole vaulter, an athletics master and a damn good runner. A few times, I've braved the chance to run with Jacqui and I've always marveled at how she can be chatting away to me while I'm barely able to breathe.

Her fitness comes from a deep love of the human body. She understands fitness and the relationship between food, movement, mindset and maintenance. Very few people are tuned into the body the way she is.

With such a deep love of health and fitness, Jacqui had always flirted with the idea of running a business that matched her passion. She'd always enjoyed teaching friends and colleagues about fitness and debunking the fad diets and workouts that come flooding through the media. As an engineer however, she wasn't sure she could jump the hurdles required to make a business successful.

Jacqui began with her pitch and discovered that people responded well to her once she had crafted her message. She communicated with clarity, credibility and real passion every time she got asked the question, "What do you do?." Pretty soon she started feeling more comfortable talking about her fitness business instead of her job.

Next she set about writing her book. Rather than a conventional book in the non-fiction genre, Jacqui wrote, *If Your Body Could Talk*, a series of letters written to you from your body. Each letter explains how the body is dealing with your daily decisions; a lot of the letters are written as a plea from the body to have a better relationship with its owner. It's fun, engaging, inspiring and informative.

The products started to take shape when we set Jacqui the challenge of creating a perfect brochure for a product she'd love her friends to buy. She created the "Love your body, Love your life" program as a twelve-week challenge for corporate women to break their sedentary lifestyle. Within a few months, she'd made enough sales to earn more each month than she was making in her corporate job.

As predictable as clockwork, a great book and a hot product generated attention, and soon she was getting press and other PR. She built her profile online and started to see new enquiries hitting her Facebook page every week.

Finally, Jacqui started looking for partnerships. She wanted people to promote her, and her book, to their contacts. She discovered that many companies had databases full of corporate women and were happy to set up strategic alliances to help more people to love their bodies and love their lives.

Today, Jacqui is looking pretty fit for business as well as for the running track. She's gained strength and power behind her brand and she can leap confidently into her new career as a fitness entrepreneur. Jacquie is a Key Person of Influence and is having an impact on people greater than she'll ever know.

**For more KPI Case Studies of people that have used this Five-Step Sequence to become more highly valued and highly paid, visit:**

*www.keypersonofinfluence.com/successstories*

# AFTERWORD

Congratulations on reading this book and taking big steps towards being a truly connected, highly regarded Key Person of Influence in the industry you love.

This book had some clear themes in it. You read about your pitch and a micro-niche, writing and publishing content, making products, becoming web-famous and developing partnerships. All of these themes are important; However, did you spot something else?

Did you notice a recurring theme that kept coming up for you? Did you connect the dots and see something valuable that you weren't expecting about your story?

When you do, you will discover that your future is clear, your past was perfect and you are present to the opportunities that are all around you.

After you spot the hidden theme, **You will get a burst of energy; you may sit up all night writing, recording, producing and playing...** and when morning comes, you're still not tired. You'll feel good because everything clicked into place.

That's because everything was for a reason. Nothing was out of order, nothing was superfluous and nothing came along to hold you back. It was all there for the purpose of letting you discover what that theme is.

If you haven't found it, you may need to read this book again. It's not the content that matters most, it's the story behind the pages. More than that, it's the chapters that are coming next that matter most.

Of course, the chapter that comes next may be at the beginning of this book as you keep looking or it may be the chapter that you write for yourself. The important thing is that you find it and it's yours to share.

# THE KEY PERSON OF INFLUENCE PROGRAM

The Key Person of Influence Program is a forty-week leadership program designed for entrepreneurs, leaders and business owners. It is designed to help you implement the five core strengths covered in this book. Thousands of people around the world have used the program to dramatically shift the performance of their business and their life.

This book stresses the importance of high quality implementation and the program is designed to manage your journey to becoming more highly valued as a Key Person of Influence in your industry.

The program runs in cities all over the world. In each city, groups of fifty-to-sixty small business owners are selected to participate in the forty-week program. The process is fast paced and results orientated. It's about implementation, not just ideas.

The Key Person of Influence program features a detailed set of best-practices. From working with thousands of people, we've discovered what creates fast results. Our method is independently recognized by the Institute of Leadership and Management, Europe's largest management training certification body. Participants receive an ILM certificate as part of their participation.

The mentors on the program are "local heroes" of business and leadership. They are typically people who have built multi-million and even multi-billion dollar companies, CEO's of big business and charities, best-selling authors and those that have sold their businesses for vast sums of money. The mentors share their real world experiences and give feedback to participants. Participants consistently tell us that the program was a catalyst for dramatic change, with the results they achieved far exceeding what they could have accomplished on their own.

For more information on the Key Person of Influence Program visit: *www.keypersonofinfluence.com/kpiprogram*

# NEXT STEPS

We offer many different resources to support you in becoming a Key Person of Influence:

**Key Person of Influence Quiz:** What you measure has a tendency to improve. This is a set of questions designed to score you on the five areas of influence described in this book. It gives you a customized report and access to training videos.
Visit: *www.keypersonofinfluence.com/quiz*

**Brand Accelerator:** This is a one day event with short, powerful keynote sessions on the five areas of influence delivered by high achieving Key People of Influence.
Visit: *www.keypersonofinfluence.com/USA*

**Facebook Page:** Go to: *www.facebook.com/OfficialKPIUSA* and join the community for some real time inspiration, updates and even more bonuses.

**Case Studies:** Model the success of some of our most successful KPIs from around the world by watching their stories on YouTube.
Visit: *www.youtube.com/user/KeyPersonOfInfluence*

**The KPI Program:** Our flagship forty-week program is ideal for established business owners, primarily in service-based industries, to reinvent themselves using the KPI Method.
Find out more, visit: *www.keypersonofinfluence.com*

# THE AUTHORS

## Kevin Harrington

Kevin Harrington – Inventor of the Infomercial, Original Shark on *Shark Tank* and *As Seen on TV* Pioneer, Best-selling author – is one of the most successful entrepreneurs in the USA. In 1980, he started The Small Business Center and Franchise America. Kevin, as a real estate and business broker, sold thousands of businesses and then offered one stop services from accounting to insurance to advertising to finance and more.

While watching television one night in 1984, Harrington noticed that at some point the only things on the screen were the color test bars that stations ran when they had nothing else to air. This gave Kevin the idea to produce the industry's first thirty-minute infomercial to fill that dead air space, which is what coined him the Inventor of the Infomercial.

Since then, he has been involved with over 500 product launches that resulted in sales of over five billion dollars worldwide and twenty products that reached individual sales of over 100 million dollars. By 1990, Harrington was named one of the 100 best entrepreneurs in the world by *Entrepreneur Magazine*.

In the mid-80's, he formed Quantum International which grew to $500 million in sales selling products in 100 countries in twenty languages. He then formed HSN Direct in conjunction with *Home Shopping Network* and soon after formed Reliant International Media. Kevin also founded As Seen on TV, Inc. and acquired AsSeenOnTV.com, the world's largest web site featuring *As Seen on TV* products.

Harrington has worked with some of the biggest celebrities including Cee Lo Green, Kim Kardashian, Paris Hilton, 50 Cent, Jack LaLane, George Foreman, Frankie Avalon, Paula Abdul, Montel Williams, Chubby Checker, Hulk Hogan, Kris and Bruce Jenner, Tony Little, Billy Mays and many more.

In 2009, Kevin was selected as one of the original *Shark Tank* Sharks on the ABC hit show. As an innovator and pioneer in the industry, Kevin has been featured on over 150 *Shark Tank* segments over the last five years on both ABC and CNBC.

Kevin is regularly featured as an industry expert in numerous media outlets including NBC *Today Show*, ABC *Good Morning America*, *CBS Morning News*, *The View*, *The Wendy Williams Show*, CNBC, *Squawk Box* with Jim Kramer, *The Bethenny Show*, Bloomberg, Fox Business, CNN, MTV, *Entrepreneur Magazine*, *Fast Company*, Fortune, Inc., *Wall Street Journal*, *New York Times* and many more.

He went on and founded two global associations – ERA (Electronic Retailers Association), which is now in forty-five countries and Young Entrepreneur's Association (now EO – Entrepreneurs Organization) which boasts combined member sales of over 500 billion dollars.

Harrington is on the board of University of South Florida (USF) entrepreneur programs and teaches regularly. He has also been involved with Moffit Cancer Research and is constantly giving back to the community. Harrington's first book, *Act Now: How I Turn Ideas Into Million-Dollar Products*, details his life and achievements in the direct marketing world, and his business was used as a class case study for twelve years at Harvard/MIT, illustrating the essential principles of grass-roots entrepreneurship.

## Daniel Priestley

Daniel founded his first company in 2002 in Australia at the age of twenty-one. Within thirteen months, the company was turning over approximately one million. In 2005, the business generated sales of over one million, after which Daniel and his partners decided to move to London.

In 2006, Daniel moved from Australia to launch an office in London. After arriving with only a suitcase and a credit card, within twelve months Daniel's business was a multi-million pound business and Daniel was considered as one of the Key People of Influence in his industry.

In 2010, Daniel released the book, *Become a Key Person of Influence*," which became a best-selling entrepreneurship book in the UK and formed the basis of a world leading growth accelerator program. In 2011, Daniel and his business partners bought Ecademy.com a technology business and social network with over 125,000 blogs and 500,000 profiles. They improved the business and sold it in under twelve months for a large profit. In 2012, Daniel released his second book, *Entrepreneur Revolution*, which became an international best-seller among entrepreneurship books.

Daniel speaks to audiences throughout Asia, Australia, Europe and the United States about business and entrepreneurship. He speaks from personal experience, spending large sums of his own money on marketing and advertising, building sales teams, recruiting and retaining high performing teams.

Daniel is passionate about social entrepreneurship and has used his businesses to raise hundreds of thousands of dollars for various charities.